D0166531

UNIVERSITY ASSOCIATES
Publishers and Consultants

SERIES IN HUMAN RELATIONS TRAINING

A Handbook of Structured Experiences for Human Relations Training

Volume IV

Edited by

J. WILLIAM PFEIFFER, Ph.D.

JOHN E. JONES, Ph.D.

University Associates, Inc.
8517 Production Avenue
San Diego, California 92121

Copyright © 1973 by University Associates, Inc.

ISBN: 0-88390-044-0

Library of Congress Catalog Card Number 73-92840

The materials that appear in this book may be freely reproduced for educational/training activities. There is no requirement to obtain special permission for such uses. We do, however, ask that the following statement appear on all reproductions:

Reproduced from
*A Handbook of Structured Experiences for
Human Relations Training, Volume IV*
J. William Pfeiffer and John E. Jones, Editors
San Diego, CA: UNIVERSITY ASSOCIATES, Inc., 1973

This permission statement is limited to reproduction of materials for educational/training events. *Systematic or large-scale reproduction or distribution—or inclusion of items in publications for sale—may be done only with prior written permission.*

Printed in the United States of America

PREFACE

In the two-and-one-half years since the publication of Volume III of *A Handbook of Structured Experiences for Human Relations Training*, we have received a great number of structured experiences from practitioners in the field of human relations. Some of these we have printed in the *Annual Handbook for Group Facilitators*, 1972 and 1973. It had been our intention to carry out the sharing of these materials through the *Annuals* alone and to end the *Handbook* series with Volume III. However, it became apparent that we had received many very important structured experiences which would only be published over a long period of time, if at all, using the *Annual* as the sole outlet. Therefore, we have chosen to resume the *Handbook* series in an effort to share a greater number of these structured experiences with other facilitators.

You will find an increased number of acknowledgements in Volume IV, since many of the experiences were created or adapted by facilitators and sent to us for consideration. It is hoped that this effort will help to dispel any concerns that the *Handbook* contains materials that rightfully "belong" to other individuals. As human relations theory and methodology grow, distinctly similar applications can be created simultaneously by two or more facilitators. Any experience that appears unacknowledged is one that we have been unable to trace to a single source, and the particular design of the experience is one that we have developed. It is the intent of University Associates to promote wide sharing of ideas, and every effort is made to give appropriate recognition to persons who develop training materials.

We are still eager to receive new structured experiences for possible inclusion in future publications, and we encourage the users of this series to submit ideas which others may find valuable in training.

J. William Pfeiffer
John E. Jones

Iowa City, Iowa
June, 1973

UNIVERSITY ASSOCIATES is an educational organization engaged in human relations training, research, consulting, publication, and both pre-service and in-service education. The organization consists of educational consultants and experienced facilitators in human relations and leadership training.

In addition to offering general laboratory experiences, University Associates designs and carries out programs on a contractual basis for various organizations. These programs fall under the following areas of specialization: Human Relations Training, Leadership Development, Organization Development, Community Development, and Educational Research.

TABLE OF CONTENTS

*Structured experiences 1-24 are contained in *Volume I;* 25-48, *Volume II:* 49-74, *Volume III;* 75-87, *1972 Annual;* and 88-100, *1973 Annual.*

INTRODUCTION

Since its inception, University Associates has become involved with or had experience in nearly every facet of human relations training. With these experiences, we have gained in our own personal growth and have found our philosophies to be continuously evolving as our awareness of the impact and methodology of human relations grows. Spontaneous experiences within a group training setting may be valuable in terms of awareness expansion and emotional freedom. However, they may not produce as much personal growth and solid, transferable learning as does a structured experience, designed to focus on individual behavior, constructive feedback, processing, and psychological integration. Our interest in providing participants with a distinctive model of human relations training has resulted in an increasing orientation within our consulting activities and offered laboratories and workshops towards experiences which will produce generally predictable outcomes. In designing human relations training experiences, we strive to become aware of and examine the specific needs of the client system or particular group and then develop learning situations which will meet these needs. We believe that this concern for learning needs should be the minimum expectation of any individual who is participating in a training event. Therefore, our training designs incorporate structure to facilitate learning.

Our initial thrust in creating learning designs led us to the increased use of what had been termed "exercises," "techniques," or "games." When the decision was made to gather these valuable materials into a book format, we became concerned that "exercise" and "game" had connotations which we considered dysfunctional to the intent of their use. We, therefore, elected to call them "structured experiences," to indicate that they are designed for experience-based learning and not merely for fun. It sometimes happens that participants have fun with structured experiences, but a major difference between games and structured experiences is that the learning goals of the latter are specifiable beforehand.

Our use of and experimentation with structured experiences have led to an interest in developing useful, uncomplicated questionnaires, opinionnaires, and other instruments. Some of these appeared in the first volume of these handbooks and have subsequently been revised and refined in later editions. Each of the volumes of the *Handbook* has contained structured experiences that include instruments. Many commercially-available instruments have found increased use in our laboratory designs, and we published *Instrumentation in Human Relations Training*, by Pfeiffer and Heslin, in June, 1973, in an effort to share the use of these materials with facilitators who had responded positively to our other publications. We find that the complementary selection of structured experiences and instruments can create powerful learning environments for participants, and we encourage those involved in the field of human relations training to become acquainted with this two-fold approach in providing for participants' learning needs.

The adaptability of both structured experiences and instruments to the creation of highly-functional training designs has emerged as a chief consideration in presenting

1

materials in published form. We have always emphasized in the *Handbook* that the material should be modified to fit the goals of the particular training group. We have occasionally suggested possible modifications ourselves. However, our awareness of the infinite variety of experiences which can be produced in adapting these materials has become more specifically focused the longer we continue to work in human relations. Therefore, we have added another section to the structured experiences format in the *Handbook* entitled "Variations." Hopefully, the variations which we suggest will trigger other adaptation ideas for the facilitator. The first three volumes of the *Handbook* are currently being revised to conform to the format of this fourth volume, and the "Variations" section will be added. In addition, we are making an effort to cross-reference experiences which supplement or compliment each other. We are also incorporating references to appropriate lecturettes and other materials from our *Annual Handbook for Group Facilitators*. The use of the "Notes" section in the *Handbook* can serve as a starting point for adaptation for the individual facilitator.

The purpose, then, of Volume IV of the *Handbook* is to share further the training materials which we have found to be viable in training designs. Part of the experiences which appear in this volume were originated within University Associates, and part were submitted to us by facilitators in the field. It is gratifying to find that facilitators around the world are using the *Handbook* and concur with the philosophy that sharing these valuable materials with others is far more in the spirit of human relations theory than the stagnating concept of "ownership" of ideas.

As in the previous volumes of the *Handbook,* the sequencing of content has been done, for the most part, in terms of the amount of understanding, skill, and experience needed by the facilitator. The first structured experience, therefore, requires much less background on the part of the facilitator than does the last. The earlier experiences generate less affect and less data than do those near the end of the book, and consequently the facilitator needs less skill in processing to use them effectively and responsibly. A concern which we bring to all of our training publications is the need for adequate processing of any human relations training experience so that participants are able to integrate the learning without the stress generated by unresolved feelings and understandings about the experience. It is at this point that the expertise of the facilitator becomes crucial if the experience is to be responsive to the learning and emotional needs of the participants. The facilitator must sort out in his own mind whether he will be able to successfully process the data which probably will emerge in the group through the structured experience. Any facilitator, regardless of his background, who is committed to growth of the individuals in his group can usefully employ these structured experiences. The choice of particular activities should be made against two criteria—the facilitator's competence and the participants' needs.

101. GETTING ACQUAINTED: A POTPOURRI

Below are listed several structured experiences that can be used as ice-breakers in human relations training events. These getting-acquainted ideas can be employed in laboratories, conferences, class meetings, and other group meetings.

1. *Superlatives.* Participants are asked to study the composition of the group quietly and to decide on a superlative adjective that describes themselves in reference to the others. (Example: youngest, tallest, most up-tight.) Then they tell their adjectives, explain, and test the accuracy of their self-perceptions.

2. *Hometown.* Secure a large blank map from a school supplies dealer. Post the map and have each participants write his first name and hometown in the proper place on the map. (As he tells about his hometown, he is disclosing important things about himself.)

3. *Demographics.* On a chalkboard, the group lists all of the background data that they would be interested in knowing about each other, such as age, marital status, educational history, etc. Participants in turn tell who they are in reference to those demographic questions.

4. *Progressive Inference.* Post sheets of newsprint on the walls, one for each participant. Group members write their first names on the sheets and then begin four rounds of self-disclosure. First, each writes his favorite English letter (A, B, C, etc.) on his sheet, returns to his seat, explains his choice, and is questioned by his fellow participants. In rounds two-four, the content is his favorite word, then his favorite phrase, and finally his favorite sentence. (Chip R. Bell, North Carolina National Bank, Charlotte.)

5. *Design.* Subgroups are formed to brainstorm getting-acquainted ideas. They select representatives who meet in the center of the room to plan an ice-breaking activity. (This meeting may be interrupted for process observations by the remainder of the group.) After a break, the representatives conduct their own design.

6. *Draw a Classroom.* Participants are given paper and pencils and are instructed to draw a classroom. They have five to ten minutes to work privately in this phase. After everyone finishes they hold their drawings in front of them and circulate around the room *without speaking* (ten minutes). Then they are asked to return to two or three interesting people to talk with them. Subgroups are formed to discuss the content of the drawings and to report to the total group. (Variations: draw an office or a shop.) (Robert T. Williams, Colorado State University, Fort Collins.)

Similar Structured Experiences: *Vol. I:* **1, 5;** *Vol. III:* **49;** *'73 Annual:* **87, 88;** *Vol. IV:* **120.**

Notes on the use of "Getting Acquainted":

102. SHOE STORE: GROUP PROBLEM-SOLVING

Goals

I. To observe communication patterns in group problem-solving.

II. To explore interpersonal influence in problem-solving.

Group Size

Teams of four to five members each. Any reasonable number of small groups may be accommodated.

Time Required

Thirty to sixty minutes, depending upon the sophistication and history of the groups.

Materials Utilized

Paper and pencils (optional).

Physical Setting

Room large enough to accommodate groups, with minimal noise interference.

Process

I. The facilitator explains to the group that they are about to perform a group task in solving a mathematical problem. He tells them that they are to arrive at consensus; that is, each member of the group must at least agree somewhat with the conclusion that has been reached by the group. Members are urged to pay attention to how the group arrives at the conclusion, so that they can later discuss the process that emerges.

II. He then states the problem as follows: "A man went into a shoe store to buy a twelve-dollar pair of shoes. He handed the clerk a twenty-dollar bill. It was early in the day, and the clerk didn't have any one-dollar bills. He took the twenty-dollar bill and went to the restaurant next door, where he exchanged it for twenty one-dollar bills. He then gave the customer his change. Later that morning the restaurant owner came to the clerk and said, 'This is a counterfeit twenty-dollar bill.' The clerk apologized profusely, and took back the phoney bill and gave the restaurant owner two good ten-dollar bills. Not counting the cost of the shoes, how much money did the shoe store lose?" (Answer: $8.00.)

(The facilitator may wish to hand out copies of this problem statement, or he may present it on a poster.)

III. When the groups arrive at a conclusion, they raise their hands, and the facilitator goes to them to ask if all are in agreement. He then asks one member to explain the process of arriving at the conclusion.

IV. The process continues until all teams have arrived at the correct answer. Groups who find the answer early may be asked by the facilitator to observe other groups, but they should be cautioned not to intervene in the problem-solving in any way.

V. The facilitator discusses the communication issues by focusing on such behaviors as the following:

1. Reacting negatively to the phrase "mathematical problem" and establishing artifical constraints.

2. Leaving the problem-solving to "experts" (self-proclaimed or otherwise).

3. Adopting pressuring tactics in reaching consensus.

4. Revealing anxiety feelings generated by observing groups who had reached the correct conclusion early.

5. Using "teaching aids" in convincing others (scraps of paper, paper and pencil, real money).

6. Feeling distress if a wrong conclusion is reached.

7. Using listening checks and other communication-skills techniques.

8. Refusing to set aside personal opinion in order to reach consensus.

VI. The facilitator may also wish to discuss the patterns of communication which were reflected in the experience. He may comment on influence behaviors, any tendencies toward one- or two-way communication modes, personal or group issues which interfered with task accomplishment, and behaviors that facilitated or were counter-productive to communication.

Variations

I. A ground rule may be established that groups may use *no* audio-visual aids. They would have to talk through the solution.

II. The problem-solving phase could begin by having individual members attempt to solve the problem independently first, before the group meeting.

III. The problem-solving discussion could be carried out via "mail" by supplying members with decks of paper slips on which they write several rounds of letters to each other. A consensus might emerge through this method, which simulates organizational problem-solving through correspondence.

IV. The problem could be acted out rather than explained orally. The skit could be videotaped so that it can easily be replayed after the consensus-seeking phase.

Similar Structured Experiences: *Vol. II:* **29, 31;** *Vol. IV:* **103, 117.**
Lecturette Source: *73 Annual:* "Synergy and Consensus-Seeking."

Notes on the use of "Shoe Store":

Submitted by Amy Zelmer, University of Alberta, Edmonton, Alberta, Canada.

103. JOE DOODLEBUG: GROUP PROBLEM-SOLVING

Goals

I. To explore the effect of participants' response sets in a group problem-solving activity.

II. To observe leadership behavior in a problem-solving situation.

Group Size

Unlimited number of groups of six (five members and an observer). Left-over members can work as process observers.

Time Required

Approximately forty-five minutes.

Materials Utilized

I. Joe Doodlebug Rule Cards (a set of five for each group).

II. Joe Doodlebug Briefing Sheets.

III. Problem-Solving Process Observation Forms.

Physical Setting

Groups are seated in circles far enough apart so as not to influence each other.

Process

I. The facilitator distributes Joe Doodlebug Briefing Sheets to members of each group. Observers are given copies of the Problem-Solving Process Observation Form.

II. After participants have had time to read the background information, he distributes Joe Doodlebug Rule Cards. Within each group each member gets a different rule card.

III. Groups are instructed to begin solving the problem in accordance with the rules. When there is substantial agreement within a group that the solution has been reached, the process observer gives a report and facilitates a discussion of how the group organized to accomplish its task.

8

IV. The facilitator solicits brief reports from each of the groups on the *process* that they developed to solve the problem. Then he asks for the *solution* from each group.

V. Group members are asked to give each other feedback, with the observer's help, on what behaviors each displayed that influenced the group.

VI. The facilitator presents a lecturette on the concept of shared leadership, stressing the responsibility of the individual member for both task attainment and group maintenance.

VII. Solution: At the moment Joe's master placed the food down, Joe had already jumped once to the east. He therefore has to jump sideways three times more to the east, and once sideways back to the west, landing on top of the food. He can eat now.

Variations

I. The problem can be made more difficult by adding redundant information.

II. The rules can be given to each member in the form of a handout.

III. Groups can be given a tight time limit of, perhaps, ten minutes.

IV. Should the groups not reach a decision after a reasonable amount of time or progress at a suitable pace, the facilitator may introject hints into the group discussion.

The hints are given as needed and as follows:

—Joe does not have to face the food in order to eat it (the facing belief).

—Joe can jump sideways and backwards as well as forwards (the direction belief).

—Joe was moving east when the food was presented (the movement belief).

V. The process described above can be followed by an original problem; that is, each group can develop a new "Joe-Doodlebug-type" problem. These can be exchanged across groups for a second round of shared leadership problem-solving.

VI. Larger groups can be accommodated, with some members having no rule cards.

Similar Structured Experiences: *Vol. II:* **29, 31;** *Vol. IV:* **102, 117.**
Lecturette Source: *73 Annual:* "Synergy and Consensus-Seeking."

This problem is adapted from a classic work by Milton Rokeach, *The Open and Closed Mind.* (New York: Basic Books, 1960.)

JOE DOODLEBUG RULE CARDS

Each of the following five rules should be typed on a 3" x 5" card. These sets are to be distributed to groups, the cards to be given out randomly within each group of five members.

Joe can jump in only four different directions: north, south, east, and west. He *cannot* jump diagonally (northeast, northwest, southeast, southwest).

Once Joe starts in any direction, he must jump *four times* in that same direction before he can change his direction.

Joe can only jump. He *cannot* crawl, fly, or walk.

Joe can jump very large distances or very small distances, but *not less than* one inch per jump.

Joe *cannot* turn around.

JOE DOODLEBUG BRIEFING SHEET

The Situation

Joe Doodlebug is a strange sort of imaginary bug that can and cannot do certain things. He has been jumping all over the place getting some exercise when his master places a pile of food three inches directly west of him. As soon as he sees all this food, he stops in his tracks, facing north. He notes that the pile of food is a little larger than he.

After all this exercise Joe is very hungry and wants to get the food as quickly as he can. He examines the situation and then says, "Darn it, I'll have to jump four times to get the food."

The Problem

Joe is a smart bug, and he is dead right in his conclusion. Why do you suppose Joe Doodlebug has to take four jumps, no more and no less, to reach the food?

PROBLEM-SOLVING PROCESS OBSERVATION FORM

Make notes in the blank spaces provided. Record *who* did *what*.

Organization   How did the group get started?

How did they begin sharing their resources?

What procedures did they develop to solve the problem?

Data Flow   How did the group get out all the information?

What data were accepted? Rejected?

How was the information collated or compiled?

Data Processing   How did the group stay on track?

What decision rules emerged?

What visual aids were employed?

How was consensus achieved and tested?

Critiquing   How did the group discuss its own functioning?

What climate emerged in the meeting?

Notes on the use of "Joe Doodlebug":

104. THE GIFT OF HAPPINESS: EXPERIENCING POSITIVE FEEDBACK

Goals

   I. To promote a climate of trust, self-worth, and positive reinforcement within a small group.

   II. To experience giving and receiving positive feedback in a non-threatening way.

Group Size

Six to ten participants who have had some experience together as a group.

Time Required

Approximately five minutes per participant and about thirty minutes for processing.

Materials Utilized

Pencils and paper.

Physical Setting

Tables or desk chairs (if not available, use lapboards or other solid writing surfaces). Participants should be located around the room so that a sense of privacy is preserved while writing.

Process

   I. The facilitator distributes pencils and paper. Each participant receives enough paper to write a message to each other member of the group.

   II. The facilitator makes a statement such as the following: "It is often possible to enjoy a small gift more than a large one. Yet, we sometimes become so concerned about not being able to do great things for each other that we neglect to do the little things that can also be very meaningful. In the following experience we will all be giving a small gift of happiness to each person in this group."

III. The facilitator then invites each participant to write on a slip of paper a message to each other member of the group. The messages are intended to make that person feel positive about himself.

IV. The facilitator recommends several possible approaches to giving positive feedback so that participants can find appropriate means of expression even for individuals whom they do not know well or do not feel close to. He may tell the participants to:

1. Try to be specific: say, "I like the way you smile at everyone when you arrive," rather than, "I like your attitude."

2. Write a *special message* to fit each person rather than a comment that could apply to several persons.

3. *Include every participant*, even if you are not too well acquainted with them. Choose whatever it is about the person that you respond to most positively.

4. Try telling each person what you have observed as his real *strength* or notable *success* in the group, why you would like to know him better, or why you are glad to be in the group with him.

5. Make your message personal: use the other person's name, state your message in the first person, and use such terms as "I like," or "I feel."

6. Tell each person what it is about him that makes you a little happier. (The facilitator may wish to distribute or post such guidelines.)

V. Participants are encouraged to sign their messages, but they are given the option of leaving them unsigned.

VI. After each message is finished, the facilitator asks the participants to fold it once and place the name of the recipient on the outside. He asks them to distribute their messages to a place designated by each participant as his "mailbox."

VII. When all messages have been delivered, the facilitator invites participants to share the feedback that was most meaningful to them, to clarify any ambiguous messages, and to express the feelings they have experienced during the process.

Variations

I. Participants may be permitted to send messages only to those persons toward whom they have significant positive feelings.

II. The content can be changed to *negative* feedback. One alternative is to have two phases, one positive and the other negative. The order of the phases can be reversed.

III. Participants can be focused on one at a time. The other members can write messages to an individual while he is predicting what feedback he will receive.

IV. The process can be generalized to include almost *any* content. Examples: "What I can't say to you is . . .," "You are the (superlative adjective) person in this group," "I want you to . . .," "I rank you ___ in closeness to me in this group because. . ."

V. Actual gifts may be exchanged as symbolic feedback. Participants can be instructed to bring to the session a personal gift that is significant to them. They may also be asked to leave the meeting to find symbolic gifts, such as flowers, stones, leaves, books, pictures, etc.

Similar Structured Experiences: *Vol. I:* **17, 18, 23;** *Vol. III:* **57, 58;** *Vol. IV:* **107.**
Lecturette Sources: *72 Annual:* "Openness, Collusion, and Feedback"; *73 Annual:* "Johari Window."

Notes on the use of "The Gift of Happiness":

Submitted by Don Keyworth, Drake University, Des Moines, Iowa.

105. WOODEN BLOCKS: A COMPETITION EXERCISE

Goals

I. To explore individual and small group goal-setting behavior and achievement motivation.

II. To study interpersonal and intergroup competition phenomena.

III. To explore feelings and outcomes of winning and losing.

Group Size

Minimum of six participants. Any reasonable number may be accommodated, given the size of the working space and the amount of material available.

Time Required

Approximately one hour.

Materials Utilized

I. About twenty stackable blocks per participant. All blocks should be the same size. The actual material and color are irrelevant. Cubes with sides of about 1½" work well.

II. Sheets of newsprint and felt-tipped marker.

III. "Prizes" for one individual and one small group.

Physical Setting

Participants are seated at solid, level tables or on a smooth-surfaced floor. Allow enough space for individuals to stack blocks without interference from others.

Process

I. The facilitator piles the blocks randomly around the work space.

II. He asks that each participant estimate silently the height of a column of blocks or number of blocks he can stack one on top of the other without having the column topple over. When each has made his estimate, the facilitator asks that each participant stack blocks and then determine whether he over- or under-estimated his ability.

III. The facilitator asks the participants to take down their columns, and he announces that they are about to play a second round of the challenge. He explains that for this round each participant will publicly announce his stacking goal and that these will be recorded for everyone to see. He also tells participants that there will be a prize for the individual with the highest estimate who completes his tower successfully. He announces that playoffs will be conducted in case of ties.

IV. When the winner has been determined and given his prize, the facilitator forms equal-sized teams of three or four, depending upon the size of the total group.

V. This time the task will be to form three columns of blocks side by side. The facilitator announces that each team will now make an estimate. He emphasizes that teams should focus on a realistic goal. He tells the teams that there will be a prize for the highest estimate completed. When the estimates have been recorded, he tells the teams to begin stacking.

VI. When the winning team has been determined and given the prize, the facilitator leads a discussion centering around influences of goal-setting behavior, group pressure and competition, willingness to assume risks, the value of external motivators (prizes), and self-imposed restrictions.

Variations

I. The facilitator may wish to add a practice round for the teams prior to their making an estimate.

II. Instead of blocks, other materials may be used, such as playing cards, tinker toys, dominoes, and pins and drinking straws.

III. The facilitator may choose to add an additional element to the competition by setting time limits on each stacking round or by noting both the time it takes teams to arrive at an estimate and the time it takes them to successfully stack the blocks.

Similar Structured Experiences: *Vol. II:* 32; *Vol. III:* 54; '72 *Annual:* 78, 81, 82, 83.
Lecturette Sources: 72 *Annual:* "Criteria of Effective Goal-Setting: The SPIRO Model"; '73 *Annual:* "Win-Lose Situations."

Submitted by Amy Zelmer, University of Alberta, Edmonton, Alberta, Canada

Notes on the use of "Wooden Blocks":

106. SCULPTURING: AN EXPRESSION OF FEELINGS

Goals

    I. To provide a nonverbal medium for the expression of feelings toward another person.

    II. To promote feedback on individual behavior.

Group Size

    Six to twelve participants.

Time Required

    Approximately forty-five minutes.

Materials Utilized

    One large sheet of paper or cardboard, at least 18″ x 24″.

Physical Setting

    A moderately-sized, comfortable room; ideally, the room in which the group has ongoing meetings. All participants, including the facilitator, are seated in a circle.

Process

    I. In the illustration here, the sculpturing intervention comes from the facilitator as part of the interaction and life of the group. If the facilitator perceives that a participant is having difficulty in expressing his feelings toward another, and if that behavior is interfering with the growth of the individual or the functioning of the group, he asks the person needing to express his feelings to stand in the center of the circle with the other participant. The individual toward whom the feelings will be expressed (A) will be told to assume the role of a lump of clay, and the participant who will be expressing his feelings (B) will assume the role of sculptor.

    II. The facilitator instructs B to sculpt A into a statue which reflects the way in which B is experiencing him and his behavior. He should give A the facial expression, gestures, and body posture which will illustrate this feedback. *A* is asked to hold the position after *B* finishes sculpturing.

III. The facilitator then instructs *B* to sculpt himself in relation to his feelings about *A* and to hold the position. He directs both *A* and *B* to reflect on their positions in relation to one another. If *A* or *B* cannot hold his position, the facilitator asks the other participants to act as "cameras" to recall gestures, postures, or expressions.

IV. The facilitator, using the sheet of paper or cardboard as an imaginary mirror, slowly moves around the statues of *A* and *B* and asks *A* to describe what he sees in the "mirror," speaking of himself first and then describing *B*. This is repeated with *B*. The facilitator may adjust the imaginary mirror if either *A* or *B* seems to be missing a significant factor in the statue.

V. The facilitator asks *A* and *B* to resume their ordinary postures. He assists *A* and *B* in talking through the experience, discussing the motivations and feelings of *B* in sculpting *A* in that particular manner and the feelings *A* was having during the experience. The facilitator may ask the group to suggest any significant behaviors which *A* and *B* overlook.

Variations

I. If the facilitator feels it is appropriate, he may ask *B* to resculpt *A* and himself as he would *like* their relationship to be.

II. The facilitator may wish to use this intervention to work through issues of concern to the whole group by asking two participants to illustrate the group issue through the sculpturing and having the group affirm or deny their perceptions of the issue.

III. The facilitator may ask the group to help model the group image, emphasis, mood, and so on. One participant stands in the center of the circle, and each other participant in turn modifies the sculpturing until there is a nonverbal consensus that the statue represents the group as it exists.

IV. Another possibility would be to employ sculpturing immediately following a dyadic experience such as the Dyadic Encounter (*Vol. I*, 21) to allow pairs to illustrate the growth of their relationship as a result of the dyadic experience.

V. All the members of a group can position themselves to form a group statue. The relative positions of the individuals can then be discussed in terms of subgroups and cohesiveness.

Similar Structured Experiences: *Vol. I:* **20, 22;** *Vol. II:* **44;** *Vol. III:* **72;** *'73 Annual:* **90.**
Lecturette Sources: *Vol. III:* **56;** *72 Annual:* "Defense Mechanisms in Groups."

Submitted by L.A. McKeown, Beverly Kaye, Richard McLean, and John Linhardt, Leadership Institute for Community Development, Washington, D.C.

Notes on the use of "Sculpturing":

107. THE PORTRAIT GAME: INDIVIDUAL FEEDBACK

Goals

I. To allow participants to receive a composite feedback picture from the members of their group as a departure from single-source individual feedback.

II. To provide an opportunity for participants to compare their individual perceptions of how the group is experiencing their behavior with the reality of the group's experience.

III. To develop skills in giving and receiving constructive feedback.

Group Size

No more than nine participants.

Time Required

A minimum of twenty minutes per participant. (Approximately two and one-half hours for a group of six participants if each wishes to participate.)

Materials Utilized

Sheets of newsprint, felt-tipped marker, and masking tape.

Physical Setting

A comfortable, intimate room with a place to display the "portraits" so that everyone can see them.

Process

I. The facilitator explains that group members will have an opportunity to request individual feedback from the entire group. They may choose to have the feedback "heavy" or "light," depending upon how comfortable they feel with receiving feedback data or the nature of the risk they are willing to take. They need neither to give nor to receive feedback if they do not wish to. He also suggests that participants can wait to make this decision after the experience has begun if they wish.

II. The facilitator chooses a secretary to write down the feedback (perhaps a member who is not willing to receive feedback at this time), or he may decide to perform this function himself. Should the secretary later decide to participate, a member who has already received his feedback could take the secretarial role for a round.

III. The facilitator asks a member who is ready to receive feedback to instruct the group to give him "heavy" or "light" feedback and to leave the room. He is instructed to make notes on what he expects to hear from the others.

IV. The facilitator explains that the rest of the group will concentrate on the member who just left the room and that they will individually verbalize their feedback when they are ready. Each statement will be written down by the secretary. He cautions the participants that they may not comment on what was said by others but that they may enlarge upon previous statements or provide comments in opposition to what has been previously stated. This brainstorming session will be halted by the facilitator after ten to fifteen minutes.

V. The facilitator invites the participant who left the room to return. He asks the participant to read the statements aloud and to ask for further explanation on certain statements if he wishes. The facilitator tells him that he may comment on individual statements or on the portrait as a whole, sharing his predictions. Interactions between the participant and the group should be allowed at this time.

VI. The facilitator asks for another participant to instruct the group and leave the room. The experience is over after all the participants who wish to take part have received their feedback.

VII. The facilitator leads a discussion of the experience, focusing on the diversity of the individual members, how it feels to receive positive or negative feedback, or other concepts relevant to the particular group.

Variations

I. The person who is the subject of the brainstorming may leave the group but stay in the room, so that he can overhear what is said.

II. Instead of brainstorming, individual remaining members may write feedback messages to the person. These may then be discussed in his absence, and a composite portrait may emerge. The individual receives the slips of paper as well as the consensus.

III. Two persons may solicit feedback on their relationship from all of the rest of the group.

IV. Casette tape recordings of the discussion may be made so that the member can later listen to what was said about him.

Similar Structured Experiences: *Vol. I:* **13, 17, 18, 23;** *Vol. II:* **38;** *Vol. III:* **57;** *'73 Annual:* **97, 99, 100;** *Vol. IV:* **104.**
Lecturette Sources: *'72 Annual:* "Openness, Collusion, and Feedback"; *'73 Annual:* "Johari Window."

Notes on the use of "The Portrait Game":

Submitted by Ferdinand Maire, Bureau de Psychologie Industrielle, Hauterive, Switzerland.

108. BALL GAME: CONTROLLING AND INFLUENCING COMMUNICATION

Goals

    I. To explore the dynamics of assuming leadership in a group.

    II. To increase awareness of the power held by the member of a group who is speaking at any given time.

    III. To diagnose communication patterns in a group.

Group Size

    Six to twelve participants. Several groups may be directed simultaneously.

Time Required

    Approximately thirty minutes.

Materials Utilized

    A ball or other convenient object for each group.

Process

    I. The facilitator explains that in the following discussion session, the manner in which the participants will interact will be limited. He tells them that possession of the ball (or other object) that he is holding will determine who may speak. He further explains that the participant with the ball must keep it until someone signals nonverbally that they wish to have it. The individual holding the ball may refuse to give it to a member who requests it.

    II. If process observers are used, they are selected and briefed.

    III. The facilitator announces a topic for the group to discuss, based upon the goals and experiences of the group. It is important to ensure that significant interaction will be generated. (Examples: silent members, expressing negative feedback, barriers to doing one's job, reactions to the training session so far.)

IV. The facilitator hands the ball to a participant, indicating that the discussion period is to begin.

V. After fifteen minutes have passed, the facilitator indicates that the discussion is over.

VI. The group processes the experience in terms of the power phenomena that emerge in reference to the holder of the ball, frustrations involved in attempting to gain or hold this power, and the patterns of communication that emerge during the experience.

VII. If process observers have been used, the facilitator asks them to provide feedback for the group.

Variations

I. The facilitator may wish to introduce a power play (or illustrate the lack of it) in the beginning by placing the ball in the center of the group rather than with an individual.

II. Participants can be given pencils and paper and be instructed to make notes to themselves on the announced topic prior to the discussion period. (This affords them the opportunity to crystallize their points of view and heightens participation.) The facilitator may direct that each participant must get the ball often enough to get all of his points into the discussion.

III. Two balls can be used, so that dyadic interaction is possible. Alternatively, the facilitator may invite participants to toss the ball back and forth in confronting each other. (This process can result in more effective listening.)

IV. A ball of string is passed around and unwound as the experience progresses, resulting in a physical sociogram or interactiongram.

Similar Structured Experiences: *Vol. II:* **48;** *Vol. IV:* **110.**
Lecturette Source: *73 Annual:* "Conditions Which Hinder Effective Communication."

Submitted by Ronald D. Jorgenson, Pacific Lutheran University, Tacoma, Washington.

Notes on the use of "Ball Game":

109. GROWTH CARDS: EXPERIMENTING WITH NEW BEHAVIOR

Goals

I. To develop an accepting atmosphere for risk-taking and self-disclosure.

II. To give those within a larger laboratory community a legitimate entry point for the provision of individual feedback to participants in other groups.

III. To supply participants with specific, individual feedback to aid them in making decisions concerning an agenda for modifying their own behavior.

IV. To increase understanding and acceptance of personality components which decrease interpersonal effectiveness.

V. To strengthen individual commitment to behavioral change through open verbalization and the development of a method or prescription for modification.

VI. To reinforce group skills of decision-making and task performance.

Group Size

This experience is specifically designed for a laboratory or workshop community, although the facilitator may wish to devise ways of adapting the structure for a single group. The exercise as presented here involves all of the participants and facilitators within a laboratory community.

Time Required

Approximately two hours.

Materials

Felt-tipped markers, 5" x 8" cards, and straight pins.

Physical Setting

One large general meeting place and the normal meeting places for the individual groups.

Process

I. The facilitator assembles the entire laboratory community to introduce the experience. He suggests that, although individuals may have been receiving feedback and interpersonal experiences through the interaction of their own groups, there is a valuable resource that has not yet been tapped—the participants in other groups within the community. He emphasizes that the goals of the human relations group experience must concern individual growth. This growth depends to a large extent on the openness, trust, and willingness of the individual participants to give and accept both positive and negative feedback. He adds that exploration of one's less effective behaviors within a group setting is often a difficult undertaking, since it involves the kind of self-disclosure that most individuals strive to avoid in their day-to-day contacts with others. However, it is the effort to become more effective interpersonally that motivates individuals to participate in human relations training experiences. Therefore, self-disclosure and feedback from others concerning negative aspects of one's personality are essential to purposeful growth.

II. The facilitator discusses the goals of this activity with the objective of instilling a commitment on the part of participants to become fully involved in the exercise.

III. The facilitator instructs the participants to return to their groups to develop behavioral prescriptions for each group member. He suggests that individuals begin by disclosing to the other members some personal characteristic which they feel is dysfunctional to them interpersonally and by stating their need for modification in behavioral terms: for example, "I ought not to apologize so often." If this selection is not seemingly appropriate to the group, then the matter is discussed by the group, and alternative suggestions are made by other participants or by the individual himself. When a final prescription is agreed upon, the group helps the individual to express it in a statement which makes *a behavioral request of other people*. For example, the request, "Help me not to be so apologetic," elicits help from others in gaining a more positive self-concept. These group-developed prescriptions are clearly written on 5" x 8" cards and pinned on the participants' clothing. (Facilitators of the groups also participate to legitimize openness and trust and to promote a sense of total community involvement.)

IV. The groups are reassembled in the large room and are asked to walk around the room, encountering as many of the other participants as possible. The facilitator emphasizes that they are not to speak during this phase. They should read each other's cards carefully and attempt to associate faces with prescriptions.

V. After a sufficient time for reading others' cards, the facilitator stops the interaction and instructs participants to form dyads. He asks them to process the experience in terms of the impact of self-disclosure and negative feedback which they experienced within their groups, feelings experienced during the milling, and their responses to each other's cards.

VI. The facilitator directs participants to leave their partners to encounter others again. He stops this interaction at some point and again asks participants to form dyads with new partners. He asks them to engage in any helping behavior with each other which seems appropriate.

VII. The facilitator announces that each dyad is to join another dyad to form quartets to process the entire experience to this point. They are to experiment with their openness and trust toward each other, giving members opportunities to engage in new behavior.

Variations

I. The facilitator may wish to increase the task component of the experience by limiting the time a group has to develop prescriptions.

II. If the groups are more oriented toward leadership than toward personal growth, the facilitator may choose to assign the quartets a task to accomplish during which members will be asked to engage in new behaviors according to their "prescribed" needs. Processing would focus on how well the modified behavior patterns facilitate task accomplishment.

III. The facilitator may wish to use an exercise such as "Analyzing and Increasing Open Behavior: The Johari Window" ('73 *Annual*, 99) as a lead-in to this experience.

Similar Structured Experiences: *Vol. I:* **13**; *'73 Annual:* **99**; *Vol. IV:* **122, 123.**
Lecturette Sources: *'72 Annual:* "Risk-Taking and Error Protection Styles," and *'73 Annual:* "Johari Window" and "Risk-Taking."

Submitted by Meyer Cahn, San Francisco State College.

Notes on the use of "Growth Cards":

110. ORGANIZATION STRUCTURES: COMMUNICATION PATTERNS

Goals

I. To demonstrate the varying effectiveness of different organization structures.

II. To diagnose working relationships within an intact group.

III. To illustrate less efficient modes of communication.

IV. To illustrate perceived alienation.

Group Size

At least eighteen participants. (See Variations section for use with smaller groups.) Several groups may be directed simultaneously.

Time Required

Approximately one hour.

Materials Utilized

I. Decks of playing cards sufficient to make up the needed number of pre-set "hands" of five cards each. Three examples of card sequences for five "players" are illustrated below. (Groups working simultaneously should receive identical sets of hands.)

Hand #	1	2	3	4	5
Cards	A♣	5♣	6♣	A♥	4♦
	2♦	Q♥	7♣	7♦	6♥
	3♥	K♥	J♣	8♦	10♣
	4♣	A♦	9♣	9♦	2♣
	Q♦	5♥	Q♣	10♦	8♥

Common element: No Spades

Hand #	1	2	3	4	5
Cards	2♣	5♥	Q♠	7♣	K♣
	3♥	3♦	4♥	10♦	K♠
	7♠	9♦	4♣	8♦	8♠
	6♦	Q♦	K♦	6♣	6♥
	J♥	2♦	J♦	3♠	4♣

Common element: No Aces

34

Hand #	1	2	3	4	5
Cards	K♥	Q♦	J♥	K♦	Q♥
	2♠	3♠	4♠	8♠	9♠
	5♥	6♥	7♥	10♥	4♥
	8♦	9♦	2♦	3♦	7♦
	10♣	A♣	5♣	6♣	2♣

Common element: Red Face Card–
King, Queen, or Jack

II. Paper and pencil for each group.

Physical Setting

A room large enough to accommodate the number of groups comfortably with flexibility for demonstrating organization structures and for creating "offices." Enough chairs should be provided so that "offices" can contain an empty chair for individuals who come in to confer with another member. The "offices" should be spaced so that conferences can be confidential.

Process

I. The facilitator announces that an experiment is to be conducted concerning organization structures. He forms three groups of five participants each (with a process observer for each group) and seats them as follows and explains the only possible communication lines as illustrated by the arrows. He may wish to post these diagrams:

Group 1   **Group 2**   **Group 3**

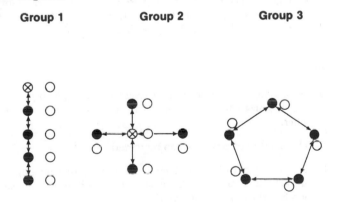

II. He announces that each group will have a problem to solve. Members will have rules to govern their communication, as follows:

1. They must go to the "office" of the person with whom they wish to confer, to talk privately without being overheard.

2. They may only speak with the person(s) previously designated with arrows in the above diagrams.

3. In Groups 1 and 2 the person in the starred position has to decide when the problem is solved, notify the facilitator, and communicate the solution. In Group 3 any member may perform these functions.

III. The facilitator distributes a hand of cards to each group member, being careful not to mix up the sets of hands, and supplies each group with a pencil and paper. He announces that, within each group, the five hands of cards have a common element. The groups must determine the common element using the communication rules previously presented. He then asks the groups to begin the task and takes note of the starting time.

IV. As soon as each group finishes, the facilitator notes the time elapsed and asks the group spokesman for the solution, in writing. Groups that finish early are instructed to sit quietly and reflect on the problem-solving process that emerged and on feelings that they experienced during this phase.

V. Each group then caucusses with its observer to reconstruct its process. After about ten minutes the total group is reassembled to discuss differences across the three groups. The facilitator announces the elapsed times and solutions for each group. The facilitator may wish to give a brief lecturette on the characteristics of the three organization structures represented—hierarchical (Group 1), leader-centered (Group 2), and radial (Group 3).

Variations

I. More than one member can be assigned to any given position. This may simulate organizational situations in which teams have to communicate with each other.

II. The number of positions can be varied.

III. The complexity of the problem can be varied by changing the number of cards in each hand or by building in a more subtle answer, such as three even-numbered cards in each hand.

IV. The nature of the problem can be changed. Even organization problems with no "correct" solution can be incorporated into this design. Such structured experiences as "Joe Doodlebug" and "Pine County" (*Vol. IV:* 103 and 117) could be used. System problems, such as absenteeism, could be explored within this activity.

V. In an intact organization, the structure of a particular group (or of the organization in which it is imbedded) can be simulated. Two possible ways to assign members are as follows:

   1. Each participant occupies his usual position in the structure (role-reinforcement).

   2. Participants are assigned to positions markedly dissimilar to their usual ones (role-reversal).

Similar Structured Experiences: *Vol. I:* **4, 12;** *Vol. II:* **28, 41;** *Vol. IV:* **108.**
Lecturette Source: *73 Annual:* "Conditions Which Hinder Effective Communication."

Notes on the use of "Organization Structures":

Submitted by Tom Irwin, Virginia Polytechnic Institute, Blacksburg.

111. SYSTEM PROBLEMS: A DIAGNOSTIC ACTIVITY

Goals

I. To generate data about the functioning of an intact group or a growth group.

II. To diagnose the way a system approaches problem-solving.

Group Size

Two groups of at least five and not more than ten participants each. (This exercise is particularly useful with "natural" groups, such as families, task groups, and committees.)

Time Required

Approximately one hour.

Materials Utilized

I. System Problems Observation Form.

II. Pencils and paper.

Process

I. The facilitator pre-selects an assertive participant and briefs him privately. The participant is told that his task is to interrupt a discussion to inject a system problem in such a way as to require the group to deal with it. Examples:

1. In a task group, the problem may be his concern about low commitment, meeting times, lack of group goals, etc.

2. In a growth group, the participant may initiate problem-solving around artificiality, uneven participation, lack of direction, etc.

3. In a family group, such problems as vacation preferences, chores, allowances, etc., may be introduced.

It is essential that the "confederate" become committed to accomplishing his task. The facilitator will assist him in eliciting a group response.

II. The facilitator places one group in the center and the other into an outer circle. (The "confederate" is a member of the inner group.) System Problems

Observation Forms are distributed to participants in the outer circle. While the observers are studying the form, members of the inner circle receive pencils and paper with which they are to make notes to themselves about a topic which the group will discuss. Suggested topics:

1. Task group: motivation, leadership style, rumors.

2. Growth group: first impressions, back-home application, openness.

3. Family group: powers of parents, house rules, discipline.

III. The facilitator participates in the inner group and initiates the discussion of the topic. After participants have become involved in the interchange, the facilitator "opens the gate" for the "confederate" to begin diverting the interaction toward the previously agreed-upon problem.

IV. When the problem is resolved or an impasse has been reached, the facilitator terminates the discussion and explains the strategy that he and the confederate used and the purposes of the intervention.

V. The facilitator asks the outer circle for process observations. Then the entire group forms one circle to talk through the experience. It is important for the facilitator to elicit comments on any feelings that participants have about being manipulated and to discuss with the group its approach to solving problems.

Variations

I. The facilitator may assign each member of the inner circle a role to play or an attitude to assume during the experience or direct each member to assume the role of another group member. For example, he could distribute role cards to each member with a brief instruction, such as, "Be reticent," "Act hostile," "Concentrate on using listening and communication skills," "Be argumentative," "Be warm and receptive to the ideas of others."

II. Have more than one "confederate," each with a different system problem. In the processing phase, the behaviors of interveners can be discussed in terms of their relative influence in diverting the task.

Similar Structured Experiences: *Vol. I:* **9, 12;** *Vol. II:* **41;** *'73 Annual:* **91.**
Lecturette Sources: *73 Annual:* "Force-Field Analysis," "Planned Renegotiation—A Norm-Setting OD Intervention."

Submitted by Morton S. Perlmutter, University of Wisconsin, Madison.

SYSTEM PROBLEMS OBSERVATION FORM

I. *Problem-Identification.* How is the problem focused by the group? Who helps to define the issue?

II. *Data-Generation.* How are points of view about the problem brought out? Whose opinions are not included in the discussion?

III. *Data-Processing.* How are various positions discussed in relation to each other? Who is influential in exploring alternatives?

IV. *Decision-Making.* How is the problem resolved? Who influences the final decision?

V. *Planning.* How are "next steps" established? Who takes responsibility for follow-through?

Notes on the use of "System Problems":

112. THE "T" TEST: AN EXPERIENTIAL LECTURE ON TRAITS

Goals

I. To introduce the concept of personality traits.

II. To illustrate the process of inferring characteristics from behavior.

III. To help diminish some of the unproductive anxiety which is often associated with filling out psychological instruments or inventories.

Group Size

Unlimited.

Time Required

Approximately thirty minutes.

Materials Utilized

I. Pencil and paper for each participant.

II. Newsprint and felt-tipped marker.

Physical Setting

Participants should be seated comfortably for writing. They should be able to see the display of group results.

Process

I. Without telling why, the facilitator announces that he is going to administer a test. He distributes pencils and paper and asks participants to get ready.

II. He tells participants the following: "For the next minute I want you to make as many T's on the sheet as you can. Make the letter T as many times as you can in one minute. Go!"

III. After one minute he says, "Stop! Now I want you to count the number of T's that you made and to write down that number.

IV. When all have finished counting, he determines the highest and lowest "score" and makes a distribution on the display chart. For example, if the highest score is 210 and the lowest score 64, he would make a chart like this:

Score Interval	Tally
201+	I
181-200	II
161-108	IHI
141-160	IHI IHI III
121-140	IHI IHI IHI I
101-120	IHI IHI IHI IHI IHI
81-100	IHI I
61- 80	II

V. He then asks, "What does this T-Test measure? It is obvious that, whatever is being measured, we don't all have equal amounts of it." Participants call out ideas about the constructs that may explain the individual differences in T-making behavior. All of these ideas are posted.

Following is a typical list of what participants hypothesize to be measured in the test:
— eye-hand coordination
— dexterity
— ability to follow directions
— creativity
— competitiveness
— T-making behavior
— anxiety
— quickness
— achievement need
— compulsiveness

VI. The facilitator initiates a discussion of the validity of the "test" (what is presumably measured by the procedure) with the participants. He leads toward a treatment of the concept of traits, which are arbitrary labels devised by psychologists to "explain" behavior by hypothesizing linear continua within people.

VII. The facilitator begins to explore the meaning of traits from a conceptual point of view. The facilitator points out that the responses offered by the group are trait-terms. In the list shown above each of the terms is generally considered a trait name, with the exception of "ability to follow directions," "eye-hand coordination," and "T-making behavior." Next the facilitator offers the following definition of traits: *"Traits are sets of categories invented by behavior-*

al scientists to permit the orderly description of behavior." From this definition a short discussion may be centered around the idea that traits do not
exist in and of themselves in the person; there is no part of the individual that
houses compulsiveness, for example. Rather, individuals respond to stimuli.
Behaviors are elicited from individuals. The person who constructs tests calls
traits into being—invents them—in an attempt to help describe behavior and
classify it within meaningful categories.

In calling a trait into being, the test-constructor or theorist must define his
trait. He does this at two levels—theoretical and operational.

A. *Theoretical Level:* the theoretical definition of a trait generally consists
   simply of the sets of words used to describe the trait. In the "T" test, for
   example, one trait name generated by the participants was that of "competitiveness." A theorist interested in the study of "competitiveness" may
   define the trait theoretically as follows: "Competitiveness is the motivation for a person to enter a structured task with the objective of out-per-
   forming all other persons engaged in the task."

B. *Operational Level:* With the above theoretical definition, it is necessary to
   develop some set of operations—an operational definition of the trait—
   in order to enable persons to respond behaviorally in such a way that the
   trait can be assessed. In the "T" test, the set of operations is the actual
   reproduction of T's on a piece of paper which merely consists of the specific behaviors employed to do the task. In and of themselves such behaviors
   have little meaning. However, when the term "competitiveness" is invented and defined, one must then elicit and measure corresponding behaviors.

Variations

I. Ask participants to record their reactions to the instructions immediately after
   the test, before scoring. (This should heighten the participation in the brainstorming of constructs.)

II. Correlate the "scores" with some demographic characteristics of the partici-
    pants. For example, tally men and women separately, or plot scores against
    age in a scatter diagram, such as follows:

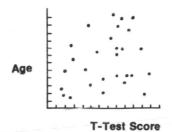

Age

T-Test Score

Structured Experience 112

III. Compare the persons with high scores with those with low scores. Encourage participants to discover other differences between the two groups.

IV. Ask participants to devise another test of competiveness (or other trait) and compare outcomes with the "T" test in terms of possible validity. Some examples:
   A. Names of countries ("World Geography Test").
   B. Circles within circles ("Concentric Patterns Test").
   C. Words beginning with the letter H ("H-Test").
   D. New uses for a brick ("The Brick Test").

V. The "T-Test" exercise can be followed by administering a commercially available instrument. Part of the processing can be focused on definitions of the traits being measured.

Similar Structured Experience: *Vol. III:* **56.**
Lecturette Source: **J. W. Pfeiffer and R. Heslin.** *Instrumentation in Human Relations Training.* **(University Associates, 1973.)**

Notes on the use of "T-Test":

Submitted by Tony Reilly, University Associates, San Diego, California.

113. GROWTH GROUP VALUES: A CLARIFICATION EXERCISE

Goals

I. To clarify one's own value system.

II. To explore values held in common within a group.

III. To study differences existing between groups.

IV. To begin to remove stereotypes held by members of different groups.

Group Size

Eight to twelve participants.

Time Required

Approximately one and a half hours.

Materials Utilized

I. Growth Group Values Worksheets.

II. Paper and pencils.

III. Newsprint, felt-tipped marker, and masking tape.

Physical Setting

Room large enough to permit subgroups to meet without interrupting each other.

Process

I. The facilitator distributes paper and pencils and directs participants to write down a group roster. The order of names is to be determined on the basis of degree of participation, as perceived by the individual member. The top name is the person perceived to be most active, and the bottom name, the participant whom he sees as least active. This ranking is carried out independently.

II. After all have finished the ranking procedure, each person in turn reads his list, while the others record the rankings that they receive.

III. The facilitator solicits each participant's reaction to the feedback which he has received on his level of participation.

IV. The facilitator then instructs the group to reach consensus (substantial agreement) on a composite rank-ordering of its membership with regard to participation. (The facilitator should carefully note the different levels of participation during this problem-solving phase.)

V. The facilitator leads a discussion of the consensus-seeking, helping members to validate the result by examining individual levels of participation during the consensus-seeking phase.

VI. Copies of the Growth Group Values Worksheet are distributed, and participants are instructed to complete the task *independently*. (Approximately ten minutes.)

VII. When all have completed the worksheet, the facilitator forms three subgroups on the basis of the composite participation rank-order (top third, middle third, bottom third).

VIII. Subgroups are asked to discover which values, as indicated on their Worksheets, are most commonly accepted and rejected among themselves. Then they discuss the implications of this in terms of their personal growth needs and their participation in the larger group's activities. (Approximately twenty minutes.)

IX. Each subgroup is asked to select a spokesman to present the findings to the total group. A *brief* summary should be rehearsed within the subgroup.

X. The total group is reassembled, and summaries are given by the three representatives. The facilitator tallies on newsprint those values most often accepted and rejected by each of the three subgroups. He leads a discussion of the results, focusing on the relationship between value systems and participation. The group is encouraged to help members to commit themselves to experimenting with new behaviors that may contribute to the accomplishment of their personal growth goals.

Variations

I. The value worksheets can be completed *before* the participant data are generated.

II. Instead of the ranking procedure outlined above, the facilitator can direct a nonverbal lineup of members on participation.

III. The ranking criterion can be varied. Participants can give each other feedback on openness, risk-taking, helpfulness, dogmatism, etc.

IV. The ranking can be changed to a rating scale, such as a five-point scale.

V. The values worksheet can be created in the group setting by asking members to write down what they believe to be the two or three predominant values that have emerged so far in the life of the group. These can be posted.

VI. The instructions to the values worksheet can be modified to include self-ratings (and one's rating of the group) on endorsement of the various values.

Similar Structured Experiences: *Vol. III:* **55;** *73 Annual:* **94.**
Lecturette Source: *73 Annual:* "Value Clarification."

Notes on the use of "Growth Group Values":

Submitted by Ord Elliott, University Associates, Iowa City, Iowa, and Dave Zellinger, Purdue University, Lafayette, Indiana.

GROWTH GROUP VALUES WORKSHEET

Directions: Place a check (✓) in front of those values which correspond to your own, and place an "X" in front of those which you personally reject. Then rank-order the *three* values which you hold most strongly by placing a "1" next to your highest value, a "2" next to your second most strongly held value, and a "3" next to your third value. Follow the same procedure for the three which you *reject* most strongly: Write a "1" next to the value you reject most, etc.

It is valuable to be:

_____ Active	_____ Explorative	_____ Sensitive
_____ Ambitious	_____ Good	_____ Spontaneous
_____ Aware	_____ Helpful	_____ Superior
_____ Better	_____ Honest	_____ Supportive
_____ Careful	_____ Influential	_____ Sure
_____ Competitive	_____ Loyal	_____ Thoughtful
_____ Considerate	_____ Open	_____ Tolerant
_____ Creative	_____ Productive	_____ Trusting
_____ Critical	_____ Right	_____ Unique
_____ Different	_____ Risky	_____ Warm

114. CLOSURE: VARIATIONS ON A THEME

Below are listed several ideas that are intended to be useful in closing human relations training events. They can also be employed for other purposes, such as fostering self-disclosure in personal growth groups. It is important to be sensitive to the amount of data which can be generated through some of the following exercises if used as "closure" experiences. Adequate time should be allocated for processing such data.

1. *Becoming.* Participants are given paper and pencils and are instructed to write their first names in large block letters on the top of the sheets. Then they are asked to complete the following sentence in as many ways as they can: "I am becoming a person who. . . ." They mill silently, reading each other's sheets, then they leave.

2. *Eye Contact Circle:* The group stands in a circle, and one member goes around the circle in a clockwise direction, establishing eye contact and verbally communicating *one-way* with each other person. He returns to his original place so that each member can tell him something. The design can be speeded up by having the second person follow the first around the circle, the third follow the second, and so on.

3. *Nebulating.* The group stands in a circle, arms around each other's shoulders. They gently sway back and forth, making eye contact with each other.

4. *Contracts.* Each participant makes a contract with one or more other persons that he will do a certain thing by a certain time. (Variation: he may write these down, with carbon copies for his own use.)

5. *Mail Boxes.* Participants are given packages of 3" x 5" cards on which they are to write final messages to each of the other group members. When all have finished, they write their first names on an extra card and take off their shoes, placing the name card in one shoe so that it can easily be read. Then they deliver their mail to the others, placing their cards in the empty shoes. They collect their mail, put on their shoes, and leave.

6. *Symbolic Gifts.* Group members verbally give each other fantasy gifts (objects, people, ideas) as a parting gesture. They may be asked to stand in front of the persons to whom they are giving gifts and to hold eye contact with them during the process.

7. *Map of Life.* On sheets of newsprint, participants draw maps of their lives, illustrating significant events. In an insert (such as is done with a more detailed map of a city on a state map) they draw a map of the current week, up to the here-and-now. Each member explains his map to the group.

8. *Think-Feel.* Participants are instructed to write on one side of a 3" x 5" card a sentence beginning with the phrase "Now I am thinking. . ." and on the other side a sentence starting with "Now I am feeling. . ." Then they are asked to interject their thoughts and feelings from both sides of their cards into a final discussion of the experience. The cards can be collected for evaluative data.

9. *Regrets.* Participants are asked to imagine leaving, getting into their cars, driving away, looking in their rearview mirrors back at the place they are leaving. They try to imagine what they would regret not having said before they left. Then they begin talking through what is left over or has not been said.

Similar Structured Experiences: *Vol. I: 23; 72 Annual: 86; Vol. IV: 104.*

Notes on the use of "Closure":

115. CONSENSUS-SEEKING: A COLLECTION OF TASKS

Goals

    I. To teach effective consensus-seeking behaviors in task groups.

    II. To explore the concept of synergy in reference to outcomes of group decision-making.

Group Size

Between five and twelve participants. Several groups may be directed simultaneously in the same room. (Synergistic outcomes are more likely to be achieved by smaller groups, *i.e.*, five to seven participants.)

Time Required

Approximately one hour.

Materials Utilized

    I. Pencils.

    II. Copies of one of the following forms:
        Life Crises Worksheet
        Dating Preferences Worksheet
        Trustworthiness of Occupations Worksheet
        Values Worksheet
        Whom to Leave Behind Worksheet
        Being a Teenager Worksheet
        Community Leader Worksheet
        Characteristics of a Good Teacher Worksheet

Physical Setting

It is desirable to have small groups seated around tables and to have the groups far enough apart so as not to disturb each other. Lapboards or desk chairs may be utilized instead of tables.

Process

I. The facilitator explains the objectives of the exercise. Each participant is given a copy of the worksheet selected by the facilitator. The task is to rank-order the items according to the instructions on the form. Participants are to work *independently* during this phase. (It is usually desirable for the facilitator to read the instructions aloud.) This step should take no more than ten minutes.

II. Groups are formed and given the task of deriving a ranking of the items by consensus. There must be *substantial agreement* (not necessarily unanimity) on the rank assigned to each item. Three ground rules are imposed in this phase:

   1. No averaging

   2. No "majority rule" voting

   3. No "horse-trading."

A number of suggestions can be made about how consensus can be achieved.

   1. Members should avoid arguing in order to win as individuals. What is "right" is the best collective judgment of the group as a whole.

   2. Conflict on ideas, solutions, predictions, etc., should be viewed as helping rather than hindering the process of seeking consensus.

   3. Problems are solved best when individual group members accept responsibility for both hearing and being heard, so that everyone is included in what is decided.

   4. Tension-reducing behaviors can be useful so long as meaningful conflict is not "smoothed over" prematurely.

   5. Each member has the responsibility to monitor the processes through which work gets done and to initiate discussions of process when the work is becoming ineffective.

   6. The best results flow from a fusion of information, logic, and emotion. Value judgments about what is best include members' feelings about the data and the process of decision-making.

The facilitator should stress that the groups should work hard to be successful. This phase should take about thirty minutes.

III. If the form used has a set of "right" answers, these are read aloud or posted by the facilitator. The score is the sum of the differences between what the correct rank is for each item and how it was ranked in the exercise. (Make all differences positive and add them up.) Participants are directed to derive the following statistics for each group: range of individual scores, average of individual scores, score for group consensus, and the difference between the average and the group consensus score.

IV. Groups de-brief the processes that emerged during the consensus-seeking phase. Discussion questions such as the following might be read by the facilitator, posted, handed out, or used by process observers:

What behaviors *helped* the consensus-seeking?
What behaviors *impeded* the process?
What pattern of decision-making occurred?
Who were the influential members? How?
How did the group discover and use its information resources?

V. Groups are brought together to publish outcomes. If there were "right" answers, summary statistics from each group are posted on a chart such as the following:

Outcome	Group 1	Group 2	Group 3
Range of Individual Scores			
Average of Individual Scores			
Score for Group Consensus			
Increment for Consensus-Seeking			
Synergy			

(In this context, synergy is defined as the consensus score being lower than the lowest individual score in the group.)

If the form does not have an answer key, the following type of chart can be used to post outcomes:

Item	Group 1	Group 2	Group 3	Row Sum	Consensus Estimate
1. (Abbreviation)					
2.					
3.					
(etc.)					

(Abbreviate the items, as labels, post the consensus rank of each group, sum across each row, and rank these sums vertically. This final ranking represents the best estimate of the consensus that would be derived if all groups combined would have done the task together.)

VI. The facilitator leads a discussion of the statistical results. He explains the concept of synergy in reference to decision-making in groups.

Variations

I. Some of these worksheets may contain cultural biases, and editing of the contents may be required.

II. Ranking forms can be developed readily both prior to the training session and during the event. For example, a list of top problems facing the organization can be written. This list can be rank-ordered by a random sample of members of the organization, and their responses can be tallied to develop an answer key. Also, within the training session, a list of items can be developed by participants to generate the content of a ranking task. A survey of all participants can be conducted to develop a set of "right" answers.

III. Groups can be encouraged to experiment with alternatives to formal voting procedures: seating themselves in the order of the way they ranked a given item as individuals, rating their agreement with each item, distributing points among alternatives, etc.

IV. The group-on-group design (Vol. I: 6) can be used to heighten participation for consensus-seeking. Two rounds can be used, with two different ranking tasks.

V. The facilitator can experiment with various group sizes. Persons can be randomly assigned to groups and given a time limit for the consensus-seeking phase. They can be asked to rate their satisfaction with the outcomes before the scoring step is begun. Average satisfaction ratings can be compared across groups and can be discussed in relation to other statistical outcomes.

VI. Similar experiments can be devised to vary time limits for the consensus-seeking phase. For example, one group can be given twenty minutes, another thirty minutes, and one no limit. Satisfaction data and outcomes can be compared. (A more complex design would be to study the effects of group size and time limit simultaneously as in the following model that requires nine groups.)

	Group Size		
Time	Small	Medium	Large
Brief			
Long			
No Limit			

VII. As an intergroup task, the same ranking form can be filled out by two separate groups. Then they can be instructed to try to predict the ranking of the other group. The two groups can be brought together to publish their actual rankings and sets of predictions. This activity gives each group a "mirror image" of itself and can lead to more effective communication across groups.

VIII. Participants can be asked to rank-order each other (independently) in terms of the amount of influence each had on the consensus-seeking outcomes. Then each participant derives a score for himself based on the differences between his ranking of the items and the consensus ranking. The average influence ranks and the deviation scores are then correlated or compared.

IX. Sequential consensus exercises can be used, so that groups build on the learnings of the process in the first phase. New groups can be formed for the second round. One task may have "right" answers, and the other may not. Other combinations are possible, such as having the group create its own instrument for the second phase.

X. The facilitator can save considerable group time and often considerable confusion by handing out two copies of the exercise form to each participant. The participant fills in both copies along with his group identification number before his group begins its discussion. He hands one copy in to the facilitator and keeps the other for his group consensus discussion. While the group is involved in developing a consensus ranking, the facilitator may find for each group: range of individual scores and the average of individual scores. This works particularly well if there are a number of staff—the task goes very quickly in this way. A chart with all the results may be made up to be shared with all the groups upon the completion of their group processing.

Answer Keys

I. Life Crises

First Level	Second Level	Third Level
1. K	4. L	10. F
2. B	5. J	11. I
3. G	6. H	12. C
	7. D	
	8. E	
	9. A	

II. Dating Preferences

First Level	Second Level	Third Level	Fourth Level
1. J	3. G	7. I	12. H
2. K	4. B	8. A	
	5. D	9. F	
	6. E	10. C	
		11. L	

III. Trustworthiness of Occupations

1. Physicians
2. Clergymen
3. Judges
4. Psychologists
5. College professors
6. Lawyers
7. Law enforcement officials
8. TV news reporters
9. Executives of large corporations
10. U.S. Army generals
11. TV repairmen
12. Auto repairmen
13. Labor union officials
14. Politicians
15. Used car salesmen

IV. Values of Young People

The items on this form are already in the correct order. (This fact is rarely discovered by participants, but it is important that it be kept

Similar Structured Experiences: *Vol. I:* **11;** *Vol. II:* **30;** *Vol. III:* **64, 69;** *'72 Annual:* **77.**
Lecturette Source: *73 Annual:* "Synergy and Consensus-Seeking."

Notes on the use of "Consensus-Seeking":

The worksheets were developed by various facilitators. The "Life Crises," "Dating Preferences," and "Community Leader" forms were submitted by Don Keyworth, Drake University, Des Moines, Iowa. The "Trustworthiness of Occupations" and "Whom to Leave Behind" worksheets were written by John J. Sherwood, Purdue University, Lafayette, Indiana. John Jones developed "Values Worksheet." "Being a Teenager" was written by Ann Dew and Suzanne Pavletich, Southeast Junior High School, Iowa City, Iowa. The authors of "Characteristics of a Good Teacher" are Ronald D. Jorgenson and Brant Holmberg, Pacific Lutheran University, Tacoma, Washington.

LIFE CRISES WORKSHEET

Introduction: Some events in our lives require significant personal and social read-justment. A recent survey asked people to rate these life crises as to the amount of readjustment they require: MAJOR, MODERATE, MILD. (Psychology Today, April 1972, pp. 71-72 & 106.)

Instructions: Rank each of the following crises events according to your estimation of how the people surveyed regarded the intensity of the event. The number of spaces given in each rank indicates the number of items to be placed there. Place the letter corresponding to each of the items in the list below in the blanks under each level.

Crisis events to be ranked under the three levels:

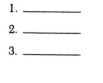

A. foreclosure of mortgage or loan
B. divorce
C. vacation
D. personal sex difficulties
E. death of close friend
F. son or daughter leaving home

G. personal injury or illness
H. pregnancy
I.   change in residence
J.   fired at work
K. death of spouse
L. marriage

First Level: *MAJOR*   **Second Level:** *MODERATE*   **Third Level:** *MILD*

1. _____   4. _____   10. _____

2. _____   5. _____   11. _____

3. _____   6. _____   12. _____

                      7. _____

                      8. _____

                      9. _____

DATING PREFERENCES WORKSHEET

Introduction: Periodically over the last decade Harvard men have been asked to rate the standards by which they chose girls for dating. They were asked to describe each characteristic as: ESSENTIAL, HELPFUL, MAKES NO DIFFERENCE, or UNDESIRABLE. (Psychology Today, Jan. 1972, pp. 65-68).

Instructions: Rank each of the following characteristics according to your estimation of their importance to Harvard men. The number of spaces given in each rank indicates the number of items to be placed there.

List of characteristics to be ranked under the four levels:

A. religious
B. well-dressed
C. altruistic
D. intellectually sophisticated
E. sexually liberated
F. socially equal

G. effervescent personality
H. unconventional lifestyle
I. good reputation
J. good conversationalist
K. sexually attractive
L. quiet personality

First Level: *ESSENTIAL*

1. _____
2. _____

Second Level: *HELPFUL*

3. _____
4. _____
5. _____
6. _____

Third Level: *MAKES NO DIFFERENCE*

7. _____
8. _____
9. _____
10. _____
11. _____

Fourth Level: *UNDESIRABLE*

12. _____

TRUSTWORTHINESS OF OCCUPATIONS WORKSHEET

Instructions: In 1971, a study was conducted at the University of Connecticut concerning attitudes toward the trustworthiness of twenty occupations. About 400 persons rated the various occupations according to the following instructions: "In their dealings with the public, can members of this occupation usually be counted on to tell the truth to the best of their knowledge, regardless of the reason? If you think they may deliberately lie or twist or distort the truth, it is not important for this rating what their reasons are." In spite of differences in age, occupations, sex, education, and locale of the raters, the respondents were remarkably similar in their assessments of the trustworthiness of the various occupations.

Below is a list of 15 occupations included in this study. Your task is to rank these 15 occupations in the same order of trustworthiness as the sample of 400 persons did. Place the number *1* by the occupation you think was ranked as the most trusted, place the number *2* by the second most trusted occupation, and so on through the number *15*, which is your estimate of the least trusted of the fifteen occupations.

_____ executives of large corporations	_____ auto repairmen
_____ college professors	_____ law enforcement officials
_____ U.S. Army generals	_____ judges
_____ clergymen	_____ politicians
_____ used car salesmen	_____ TV repairmen
_____ physicians	_____ psychologists
_____ labor union officials	_____ TV news reporters
_____ lawyers	

VALUES WORKSHEET

Instructions: Complete the following sentences in your own words. Then compare your responses to those of the other members of your group in order to generate a set of commonly held values in interpersonal relations. In the discussion you have four tasks: (1) to make yourself heard, (2) to hear others accurately, (3) to listen for themes, and (4) to collaborate on the group consensus.

People should...

People should never...

A boss...

A subordinate...

A friend...

A spouse...

I get excited when...

I want to be remembered as a person who...

The most worthwhile thing a person could do is...

WHOM TO LEAVE BEHIND WORKSHEET

Instructions: The ten persons listed below have been selected as passengers on a
space ship for a flight to another planet because tomorrow the planet Earth is
doomed for destruction. Due to changes in space limitations, it has now been
determined that only seven persons may go. Any seven qualify.

Your task is to select the seven passengers. There are therefore *three* persons
now on the list who will not go. Place the number *1* by the person you think should
be *removed first* from the list of passengers; place the number 2 by the person
you think should be removed second from the list; and, finally, place the number
3 by the person you think should be removed third from the list. Choose *only
three*. These are the three persons who will not make the trip. They are to be
left behind.

_____ An accountant   _____ A Negro medical student

_____ The accountant's   _____ A famous novelist
          pregnant wife

_____ A liberal arts coed   _____ A biochemist

_____ A professional   _____ A 70-year-old clergyman
          basketball player

_____ An intelligent female   _____ An armed policeman
          movie star

BEING A TEENAGER WORKSHEET

Instructions: You are asked to rank the following statements. Place a number "1" to the left of the statement you decide is the most correct about teenagers. The next most correct statement would be number "2," and the least correct would be marked as number "8."

_____ A. The opinions of teenagers are equally as important as those of their parents.

_____ B. If there are any changes or reforms made in society, they will come from today's vocal teenagers, rather than from adults.

_____ C. Being a teenager is a safe age—you aren't expected to behave like an adult, but you aren't treated like a child.

_____ D. Advice from friends is worth more than advice from parents.

_____ E. Being a teenager has its advantages and disadvantages, just like any other age group.

_____ F. Time is the only thing in a teenager's favor. If you can just wait out the years until you are twenty, then it will be easy going.

_____ G. This country will be better off if today's teenagers will end up being like their parents.

_____ H. What teenagers really want is to be able to voice their opinions and make their own decisions.

COMMUNITY LEADER WORKSHEET

Instructions: Below is a list of characteristics which might be used to describe a community leader. Your task is to select from this list the five characteristics which you feel are the most important for a community leader and to rank the five characteristics in order of importance (1 is most important; 5, least important).

Which five of the following characteristics are most important for a community leader?

_____ initiative   _____ generalized experience

_____ interest in people   _____ specialized experience

_____ well organized   _____ sense of humor

_____ awareness of local   _____ good socializer
              politics

_____ intelligence   _____ respect in community

_____ emotional stability   _____ financial independence

_____ cultural interests   _____ physical health and vigor

_____ loyalty to community   _____ grasp of local issues

CHARACTERISTICS OF A GOOD TEACHER WORKSHEET

Instructions: Your task is to rank the items below as you perceive them in order of importance from 1 to 10, one being the most important characteristic. It may be helpful if you proceed from 1 (most) to 10 (least), 2 (second-most) to 9 (second-least), etc.

After each of you has made a ranking, you will then be asked to form into designated groups and discuss the items below until you arrive at consensus about the importance of the items as *you* see them.

Your Ranking	Ranking by Group Consensus	
(____)	(____)	The teacher's classes are usually well-disciplined and orderly.
(____)	(____)	The teacher uses many methods to keep in touch with how pupils feel about his/her teaching, their work, and themselves.
(____)	(____)	The teacher sets high standards of academic achievement and does not allow sloppy, careless work to get by.
(____)	(____)	The teacher admits his/her own errors to pupils openly and easily.
(____)	(____)	The teacher allows pupils (individually and as a group) to make many decisions about their activities, their use of time, and their room.
(____)	(____)	Other teachers report he/she is helpful, cooperative, and stimulating to work with.
(____)	(____)	Parents report that their conferences with him/her are valuable and enlightening.
(____)	(____)	The teacher keeps up to date on the subject matter of anything he/she teaches.
(____)	(____)	The teacher's pupils discuss almost anything with him/her without fear or hesitation.
(____)	(____)	The teacher places great emphasis upon pupils learning to work together effectively and to understand each other.

Structured Experience 115

116. DIALOG: A PROGRAM FOR DEVELOPING WORK RELATIONSHIPS

Goals

I. To increase openness in work relationships.

II. To generate higher trust in interpersonal relations in work settings.

III. To clarify assumptions that persons who work together make about each other and each other's jobs.

Group Size

Any number of paired participants.

Time Required

A minimum of two hours. (May be scheduled at two different times.)

Materials Utilized

One reusable Dialog booklet for each participant. The booklet should be prepared in such a way that participants are presented statements one at a time. The format which follows illustrates how each page should look. (Copies of pre-assembled Dialog booklets may be ordered from University Associates. The price is fifty cents each, and the minimum order is twelve copies.)

Physical Setting

Pairs of participants are instructed to find a private place somewhere in the immediate vicinity, such as in other rooms or out of doors.

Process

I. The facilitator introduces the experience by discussing how work relationships are enhanced by self-disclosure and feedback.

II. Participants are paired by any appropriate method. (Sample criteria: boss-subordinate, new-old employees, natural work pairs, persons who do not know each other very well.)

III. A copy of the Dialog booklet is given to each participant, and the pairs are instructed to find a private place to work through the exercise. An announcement is made concerning when the total group is to reassemble.

IV. After the paired activity, the total group reassembles. The facilitator assists in the processing of the event by encouraging participants to share what they learned about *themselves* through the experience. (Remember that a ground rule of confidentiality is established by the directions.)

Variations

I. The Dialog exercise can be used in conjunction with the Dyadic Encounter booklets (*Vol. I:* 21). The two structured experiences can be incorporated into the same laboratory design to build on each other.

II. The event can be divided into two periods by stopping the discussion at the end of page 24. Two one-hour sessions can be scheduled at different times.

III. Participants can be given paper and pencils and be instructed to write out their responses to the "mirroring" items: pages 7, 11, 16, 23, 28, 33, 34, 38, 39, and 42. These pages have the letter "M" printed after the page number.

IV. A "third party" can be used as a process facilitator to the pair who are going through the Dialog booklet. The extra person assists the two in listening, expressing themselves, and responding to each other. He also facilitates the intermittent processing of the experience. (This design is somewhat analogous to marriage counseling, and this is one application of the Dialog materials.)

V. The exercise can be used in interviewing prospective employees, orienting new employees, establishing temporary work relationships, building intact work teams, and building laboratory staffs.

VI. Items from the Dialog booklet may be posted on newsprint to stimulate group discussion. Subgroups may be formed to exchange responses to selected items as an ice-breaking activity in a laboratory or workshop.

VII. The facilitator can experiment with various group sizes in using this structured experience. Triads, quartets, etc., can be established, but this option may require more time.

Similar Structured Experiences: *Vol. I:* **21;** *Vol. II:* **45;** *Vol. III:* **70;** *Vol. IV:* **118.**
Lecturette Sources: *72 Annual:* "Openness, Collusion, and Feedback"; *73 Annual:* "Johari Window."

Submitted by John E. Jones, University Associates, Iowa City, and Johanna J. Jones, University of Iowa, Iowa City.

Structured Experience 116

Notes on the use of "Dialog":

DIALOG

**A Program for Developing
Work Relationships**

2

Read silently. Do not look ahead in this booklet.

The conversation which you are about to begin is intended to point toward more effective human relations in a work setting. Tasks are accomplished more effectively if persons who work together have the capacity to exchange ideas, points of view, feelings, attitudes, and opinions freely. It is also important that you be able to clarify assumptions that you make about each other in relation to the work to be done.

3

The basic purpose of the discussion which you are about to have is to foster greater understanding of each other at work. By telling about oneself and by sharing perceptions of each other you will be working toward a higher level of trust.

These ground rules should be followed:

1. Take turns initiating the discussion. The program consists of a series of open-ended statements. Each of you should complete each statement orally. (Do not write in the booklet.)
2. All of this discussion is confidential.
3. Do not look ahead in the booklet.
4. Do not skip items. Respond to each one in the order in which it is presented.

When each of you has finished reading, turn the page and begin.

4

Basically my job is...

5

Usually I am the kind of person who...

6

When things aren't going well I...

Structured Experience 116

7M

When I think about your responsibilities I think that...

8

I want to become the kind of person who...

9

I like such things as...

10

The most important skill in developing work relationships is listening. To begin improving your ability to hear each other, follow these steps: complete the following item in two or three sentences; the listener then repeats *in his own words* what you said; then the listener completes the item, and you paraphrase what you heard.

Ten years from now I...

When each of you has had a turn, share what you may have learned about listening.

During this discussion, you may wish to continue the development of your listening by using the phrase, "What I hear you saying is..."

11M

My first impression of you was...

12

On the job I'm best at...

13

My greatest weakness on the job is...

14

In conflict situations between people I usually...

Briefly discuss how this exchange is developing.

15

When I am supervising someone, I prefer...

16M

Your job seems to be...

17

The best boss I ever had...

18

The best supervisee (or colleague) I ever had...

Listening check: "What I hear you saying is..."

19

The worst boss I ever had...

20

The worst supervisee (or colleague) I ever had...

Have a brief discussion of what your responses to the last four items say about what you believe to be valuable in work relationships. Draw generalizations about each other.

21

I usually react to negative criticism by...

22

When I am approaching a deadline, I...

23M

What I like about you is...

Structured Experience 116

24

This conversation ...

25

I joined this organization because ...

26

During the past few months I've been ...

Listening check: "What I hear you saying is ..."

27

The next thing I'm going to try to accomplish is ...

28M

My general image of you is ...

29

I prefer to get feedback ...

30

As a member of a team I ...

31

I prefer to work with people who ...

32

Right now I'm feeling ...

33M

What puzzles me about you is ...

34M

I am imagining that you...

35

The next step in my career development seems to be...

36

The person I'm having the most trouble with...

Have a brief discussion of how this conversation is going so far. How open are you being? How do you feel about your participation up to this point?

37

I need to...

38M

Faced with a choice between the goals of the organization and your own welfare, I would predict that you would...

39M

Here's an actual situation in which I was involved. (Explain.)
What do you think I did? How do you think I felt?

40

I'd like to get you involved in...

41

I'm hoping that...

Listening check: "What I hear you saying is..."

42M

I think you see me as . . .

43

If I could just . . .

44

My position in this organization . . .

45

My own personal goals are to . . .

46

You and I can . . .

Have a brief discussion of your reactions to this conversation.

47

This discussion was intended to open up a dialog which should be carried on continuously in your work relationship. You may wish to make definite plans to continue this exchange in the future. Some activities which you may consider are the following:

Go through this Dialog booklet again after about six months.
Make your relationship an agenda item in each meeting.
Contract with each other for support in changing your behavior at work.
Work through this exchange with other people with whom you work.

117. PINE COUNTY: INFORMATION-SHARING

Goals

I. To explore the effects of collaboration and competition in group problem-solving.

II. To study how task-relevant information is shared within a work group.

III. To observe problem-solving strategies within a group.

IV. To demonstrate the impact of various leadership styles on task accomplishment.

Group Size

Unlimited number of groups of five participants each. These groups may be directed simultaneously in the same room.

Time Required

Approximately one hour.

Materials

I. A set of five Pine County Data Sheets for each group of participants. (Each sheet contains unique data and is coded by the number of periods, from one to five, following the last sentence of the first paragraph.)

II. Pine County Candidate Summary Sheet for each participant.

III. Pine County Briefing Sheet for each participant.

IV. Pine County Solution Sheet for each participant.

V. Sheets of newsprint, felt-tipped markers, masking tape, and pencils may be made available to groups.

Physical Setting

One room large enough so that the individual groups of five can work without being disrupted by other groups and without being influenced by problem solutions overheard from other groups. An alternative setting would be a room large enough to hold all participants comfortably during the instructions and processing phases and several smaller rooms where individual groups could work undisturbed during the problem-solving phase. It is useful for groups to work at tables. Supply extra chairs near the groups if observers are used.

Process

I. The facilitator explains to the participants that they will be doing an exercise in problem-solving. He should not, however, suggest in his introduction any clue or key to the problem-solving.

II. The facilitator forms groups of five participants by any convenient and appropriate method. If he wishes to use observers, he assigns them to groups or suggests that they move from group to group. (The first method provides individual feedback on work styles, and the second method provides generalizable data concerning behavior in task groups.)

III. The facilitator explains that each group's task is to select a director for the Family Counseling Unit of the Community Action Agency. He indicates that there is only one correct solution, and he cautions them that each group must reach its solution independently. He indicates that when each group has completed the problem-solving and has given its solution to him, participants may observe other groups still in process. They may not, however, join another group or influence another group's process in any way.

IV. The facilitator then distributes Candidate Summary Sheets, Briefing Sheets, and individual Data Sheets to each participant, taking care that all five differently coded Data Sheets (number of periods at the end of the first paragraph) have been distributed in each group. (If observers are used, they may be briefed outside the main room.)

V. The groups begin the problem-solving process when the facilitator gives the signal. Groups are given the expectation that they will be able to reach a solution within thirty minutes. He may incorporate an element of competition by posting the number of minutes used by each group in solving the problem.

VI. When all groups have found a solution to the problem, the facilitator and/or the observers initiate a discussion of the problem-solving processes observed in the groups, focusing on strategies employed, the effects of collaboration and competition, noncontributing participants, and the importance of the information-sharing process.

VII. Pine County Solution Sheets are distributed and discussed.

VIII. To generalize upon the importance of examining the significance of all members' input, the facilitator may wish to use the following diagram:

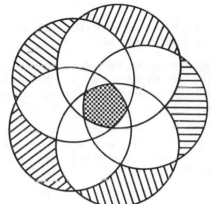

Shaded area represents common knowledge, i.e., knowledge or experience possessed by each member of the group.

Crosshatched area represents an area of knowledge or experience peculiar to only one member of the group.

Unmarked but enclosed area represents an overlapping of knowledge or experience shared by two or more members of the group.

Group decisions are more likely to be effective if they result from discussions that draw upon information known by each individual, information shared by combinations of individuals, and information that is common to all group members.

Note: Occasionally, a group will not be able to solve the problem within the time limitations (approximately thirty minutes, with some extension at the facilitator's discretion), and he may have to intervene and stop the process so that there is adequate time to discuss the experience. Sometimes, when a group has failed to arrive at the correct solution, members will exhibit a defensive reaction and attack the facilitator for "manipulation," that is, structuring the task so that the group was destined to fail. This feedback needs to be explored, and the facilitator should keep the following points in mind:

1. Participants were given no false, misleading, or conflicting information.

2. The facilitator did not attempt to influence the way in which the group attempted to solve the problem.

3. Their attack may be a defense employed to keep from dealing with the behavioral feedback generated by the exercise.

Variations

I. The worksheets may be rewritten to contain material more specific to the particular participant group. The formula is simple: begin at the end, with a

Structured Experience 117

correct solution, and apportion data to participants so that each has a critical piece of information as well as common knowledge.

II. Additional participants can be accommodated within the groups by duplicating data sheets. For example, if there are seven members, two participants receive the sheet with one period at the end of the first paragraph, and two receive the sheet with two periods.

III. The problem-solving phase can be interrupted several times for processing. Observers can be instructed to give descriptive reports to the groups which they are observing. Participants can be instructed to rate their confidence in the correctness of the solution and their satisfaction with the work style of the group.

IV. The event may be "staged" in a group-on-group arrangement, so that one group of five solves the problem and the other group (which may be any size) observes. The problem-solving can be interrupted from time to time for process observations. Observers can be assigned different aspects of the process. Observers can be divided into subgroups sporadically to diagnose the functioning of the task group.

Similar Structured Experiences: *Vol. II:* **31;** *'72 Annual:* **80;** *Vol. IV:* **103, 107.**

Notes on the use of "Pine County":

Submitted by Lawrence Dunn, Training and Development Systems, Ltd., Boston.

PINE COUNTY DATA SHEET

The Pine County Family Counseling Unit provides services in relation to family problems, mental health difficulties, child-school relationships, etc. The Community Action Agency (CAA), of which the unit is a part, is governed by policies which are generally established by its Board. However, as a concession to social service programs funded by the Community Fund and the Community Chest, the CAA has agreed that its salary categories will be in line with those of other service groups in the community.

Pine County was once a prosperous community, which, because of employment opportunities, attracted people of many diverse backgrounds. The depletion of timber and mineral resources and technological change has now severely undermined the economy. Today there is much unemployment, and the Department of Welfare provides limited assistance to many persons. The recently-established Pine County Family Counseling Unit has never been able to cope adequately with the many requests for its help. The CAA Board, therefore, is placing great stress on the selection of a strong director who, it is hoped, will be able to improve the CAA's social service component.

The director is expected to participate in CAA Board meetings, to carry responsibility for community and other Agency relations, and to oversee the Agency's services. The CAA Board has ruled that the director must have passed the thirtieth birthday, have at least three years of supervisory or administrative experiences, and hold a degree of Master of Social Work (MSW). It has also ruled that he must have had a course in casework.

The Pine County CAA's Family Counseling Unit maintains four service centers: Hilldale, with offices for the director and assistant director, Nogulch, Farout, and Lastreach. The Hilldale center is located in the county seat and is staffed by five case aides and a supervisor, who doubles as assistant director. At Nogulch, some fifteen miles to the north, there is a supervisor with four case aides. The Nogulch supervisor joined the Agency eight years ago after fifteen years of employment in the Department of Welfare. At Lastreach, there are three case aides and a supervisor, who joined the Agency staff in the fall of 1969 after receiving an MSW degree from Pacific Slopes. The staff at Farout consists of three case aides and a supervisor, who came to the Agency nine years ago as a case aide and was promoted to his present position after obtaining supplementary training.

There are a number of schools offering the MSW degree, the most recently accredited being Pacific Slopes, which reorganized and expanded its department in 1969 to include group work. Its course requirements consist of family problems, casework, group methods, and agency management.

PINE COUNTY DATA SHEET

The Pine County Family Counseling Unit provides services in relation to family problems, mental health difficulties, child-school relationships, etc. The Community Action Agency (CAA), of which the unit is a part, is governed by policies which are generally established by its Board. However, as a concession to social service programs funded by the Community Fund and the Community Chest, the CAA has agreed that its salary categories will be in line with those of other service groups in the community..

Pine County was once a prosperous community, which, because of employment opportunities, attracted people of many diverse backgrounds. The depletion of timber and mineral resources and technological change has now severely undermined the economy. Today there is much unemployment, and the Department of Welfare provides limited assistance to many persons. The recently established Pine County Family Counseling Unit has never been able to cope adequately with the many requests for its help. The CAA Board, therefore, is placing great stress on the selection of a strong director who, it is hoped, will be able to improve the CAA's social service component.

The director is expected to participate in CAA Board meetings, to carry responsibility for community and other Agency relations, and to oversee the Agency's services. The CAA Board has ruled that the director must have passed the thirtieth birthday, have at least three years of supervisory or administrative experience, and hold a degree of Master of Social Work (MSW) from an accredited school.

The County CAA's Family Counseling Unit maintains four service centers: Hilldale, with offices for the director and assistant director, Nogulch, Farout, and Lastreach. The Hilldale center is located in the county seat and is staffed by five case aides and a supervisor, who doubles as assistant director. At Nogulch, some fifteen miles to the north, there is a supervisor with four case aides. The Nogulch supervisor joined the Agency eight years ago after fifteen years of employment in the Department of Welfare. At Lastreach, there are three case aides and a supervisor who joined the Agency staff in the fall of 1969 after receiving an MSW degree from Pacific Slopes. The staff at Farout consists of three case aides and a supervisor, who came to the Agency nine years ago as a case aide and was promoted to his present position after obtaining supplementary training.

There are a number of schools offering an MSW degree, but a passing grade in a course in casework is essential to qualify for membership in the United States Federation of Social Service Workers. The largest school is Eastern Shores, which includes among its requirements courses in family problems, casework, group methods, and agency management. The smallest is not accredited.

PINE COUNTY DATA SHEET

The Pine County Family Counseling Unit provides services in relation to family problems, mental health difficulties, child-school relationships, etc. The Community Action Agency (CAA), of which the unit is a part, is governed by policies which are generally established by its Board. However, as a concession to social service programs funded by the Community Fund and the Community Chest, the CAA has agreed that its salary categories will be in line with those of other service groups in the community...

Pine County was once a prosperous community, which, because of employment opportunities, attracted people of many diverse backgrounds. The depletion of timber and mineral resources and technological change has now severely undermined the economy. Today there is much unemployment, and the Department of Welfare provides limited assistance to many persons. The recently established Family Counseling Unit has never been able to cope adequately with the many requests for its help. The CAA Board, therefore, is placing great stress on the selection of a strong director, who, it is hoped, will be able to improve the CAA's social service component.

The director is expected to participate in CAA Board Meetings, to carry responsibility for community and other Agency relations, and to oversee the Agency's services. The CAA Board has ruled that the director must have passed the thirtieth birthday, have at least three years of supervisory or administrative experience, and hold a degree of Master of Social Work (MSW).

The Pine County CAA's Family Counseling Unit maintains four service centers: Hilldale, with offices for the director and assistant director, Nogulch, Farout, and Lastreach. The Hilldale center is located in the county seat and is staffed by five case aides and a supervisor, who doubles as assistant director. At Nogulch, some fifteen miles to the north, there is a supervisor with four case aides. The Nogulch supervisor joined the Agency eight years ago after fifteen years of employment in the Department of Welfare. At Lastreach, there are three case aides and a supervisor, who joined the Agency staff in the fall of 1969 after receiving an MSW degree from Pacific Slopes. The staff at Farout consists of three case aides and a supervisor, who came to the Agency nine years ago as a case aide and was promoted to his present position after obtaining supplementary training. He is known to have severe problems in accepting suggestions from women.

There are a number of schools offering an MSW degree, and a passing grade in a course in family problems is essential to qualify for membership in the United States Federation of Social Service Workers. Western Seas is one of the oldest schools and includes among its requirements courses in family problems, casework, group methods, and agency management. Course requirements at Lonely Pines, the smallest, include family problems, casework, and group methods.

PINE COUNTY DATA SHEET

The Pine County Family Counseling Unit provides services in relation to family problems, mental health difficulties, child-school relationships, etc. The Community Action Agency (CAA), of which the unit is a part, is governed by policies which are generally established by its Board. However, as a concession to social service programs funded by the Community Fund and the Community Chest, the CAA has agreed that its salary categories will be in line with those of other service groups in the community . . . .

Pine County was once a prosperous community, which, because of employment opportunities, attracted people of many diverse backgrounds. The depletion of timber and mineral resources and technological change has now severely undermined the economy. Today there is much unemployment, and the Department of Welfare provides limited assistance to many persons. The recently established Family Counseling Unit has never been able to cope adequately with the many requests for its help. The CAA Board, therefore, is placing great stress on the selection of a strong director who, it is hoped, will be able to improve the CAA's social service component.

The director is expected to participate in CAA Board meetings, to carry responsibility for community and other Agency relations, and to oversee the Agency's services. The CAA Board has ruled that the director must have passed the thirtieth birthday, have at least three years of supervisory or administrative experience, and hold a degree of Master of Social Work (MSW). He must also be a member of the United States Federation of Social Service Workers (USFSSW).

The Pine County CAA's Family Counseling Unit maintains four service centers: Hilldale, with offices for the director and assistant director, Nogulch, Farout, and Lastreach. The Hilldale center is located in the county seat and is staffed by five case aides and a supervisor, who doubles as assistant director. This individual holds an MSW granted in 1969 by Southern University for Negro Women. At Nogulch, some fifteen miles to the north, there is a supervisor with four case aides. The Nogulch supervisor joined the Agency eight years ago after fifteen years of employment in the Department of Welfare. At Lastreach, there are three case aides and a supervisor, who joined the Agency staff in the fall of 1969 after receiving an MSW degree from Pacific Slopes. The staff at Farout consists of three case aides and a supervisor, who came to the Agency nine years ago as a case aide and was promoted to his present position after obtaining supplementary training.

There are a number of schools offering an MSW degree, and membership in the United States Federation of Social Service Workers can be obtained without formality by graduates of accredited schools. Southern Comfort, which is not the smallest school, includes the following among its requirements: family problems, casework, and group methods.

PINE COUNTY DATA SHEET

The Pine County Family Counseling Unit provides services in relation to family problems, mental health difficulties, child-school relationships, etc. The Community Action Agency (CAA), of which the unit is a part, is governed by policies which are generally established by its Board. However, as a concession to social service programs funded by the Community Fund and the Community Chest, the CAA has agreed that its salary categories will be in line with those of other service groups in the community.....

Pine County was once a prosperous community, which, because of employment opportunities, attracted people of many diverse backgrounds. The depletion of timber and mineral resources and technological change has now severely undermined the economy. Today there is much unemployment, and the Department of Welfare provides limited assistance to many persons. The recently established County Family Counseling Unit has never been able to cope adequately with the many requests for its help. The CAA Board, therefore, is placing great stress on the selection of a strong director who, it is hoped, will be able to improve the CAA's social service component.

The director is expected to participate in CAA Board meetings, to carry responsibility for community and other Agency relations, and to oversee the Agency's services. The CAA Board has ruled that the director must have passed the thirtieth birthday, have at least three years of supervisory or administrative experience, and hold a degree of Master of Social Work (MSW). It has also ruled that the candidate's training must have included work in group methods.

The Pine County CAA's Family Counseling Unit maintains four service centers: Hilldale, with offices for the director and assistant director, Nogulch, Farout, and Lastreach. The Hilldale center is located in the county seat and is staffed by five case aides and a supervisor, who doubles as assistant director. At Nogulch, some fifteen miles to the north, there is a supervisor with four case aides. The Nogulch supervisor joined the Agency eight years ago after fifteen years of employment in the Department of Welfare. At Lastreach, there are three case aides and a supervisor, who joined the Agency staff·in the fall of 1969 after receiving an MSW degree from Pacific Slopes. The staff at Farout consists of three case aides and a supervisor, who came to the Agency nine years ago as a case aide and was promoted to his present position after obtaining supplementary training.

There are a number of schools offering the MSW degree. A degree from an accredited institution is necessary to qualify for membership in the United States Federation of Social Service Workers. The smaller U.S. schools require three, the larger four, of the following subjects: family problems, casework, group methods, and agency management.

Structured Experience 117

PINE COUNTY CANDIDATE SUMMARY SHEET

J. BLACK

Personal	Born March 3, 1940, New York Married, 2 children
Education	Eastern Shores, MSW, 1963
Employment	Caseworker, New York Dept. of Welfare, 1963-65 Lecturer in Casework, Eastern Shores, 1966-71 Supervisor, New York Children's Agency, 1971-

L. GREEN

Personal	Born December 30, 1943, Baltimore Married, 3 children
Education	Southern Comfort, MSW, 1968
Employment	Caseworker, Family Service Agency, 1966-68 Supervisor, Children's Aid, 1968-70 Supervisor, Family Service Agency, 1970-

R. WHITE

Personal	Born June 15, 1937, Los Angeles Married, no children
Education	Pacific Slopes, MSW, 1967
Employment	Parole Officer, Idaho Parental School, 1967-70 Chief Probation Officer, 1970-

A. RED

Personal	Born January 10, 1939, Chicago Married, 1 child
Education	Western Seas, MSW, 1967
Employment	Caseworker, Children's Agency, Chicago, 1967-68 Caseworker, Family Welfare Society, Urbana, 1968-69 Case Supervisor, Family Welfare Society, Urbana, 1969-

B. GRAY

Personal	Born January 15, 1938, Middletown, New York Married, 1 child

Education	National School of Social Services, London, United Kingdom, MSW, 1966
Employment	Caseworker, Lutheran Family Service, 1966-68 Lecturer, Southern Comfort, 1968-69 Director, Lutheran Family Service, 1969-

H. BROWN

Personal	Born March 3, 1937, Des Moines Single
Education	Lonely Pines, MSW, 1962
Employment	Parole Officer, Big Mound Detention Center, 1962-66 Counselor, Children's Mental Health Center, 1966-68 Director, Western County Center for Girls, 1968-

PINE COUNTY BRIEFING SHEET

Instructions

1. You are a member of the personnel committee of the Pine County Community Action Agency. Your committee consists of Board and Staff representatives.

2. You are meeting to select a candidate from a list who, upon Board action, will become the Director of the Family Counseling Unit.

3. The data you bring with you (Pine County Data Sheet) are in your head. *You may not exchange data sheets.*

4. There is one correct solution.

5. All data are correct.

6. You have approximately thirty minutes to choose the candidate.

7. Assume that today's date is August 1, 1973.

8. There must be substantial agreement when the problem has been solved.

9. You must solve the problem as a group.

10. You may organize your work in any way you wish.

11. You are free to use any material resources in the room.

PINE COUNTY SOLUTION SHEET

	BLACK	GREEN	WHITE	RED	GRAY	BROWN
Age:	33	29	36	34	35	37
Educ.:	Eastern Shores	Southern Comfort	*Pacific Slopes*	Western Seas	*National School, UK*	*Lonely Pines*
Exper:	*2 years*	5 years	3 years	4 years	4 years	5 years

BLACK has only two years of supervisory experience.

GREEN is only 29 years of age.

WHITE received an MSW from Pacific Slopes in 1967, when the school was not accredited.

GRAY did not attend a U.S. school and therefore does not qualify for membership in the United States Federation of Social Service Workers.

BROWN obtained an MSW from Lonely Pines. Lonely Pines is the smallest school and not, therefore, accredited.

RED is the choice, because only he meets all the requirements.

118. TWENTY-FIVE QUESTIONS: A TEAM DEVELOPMENT EXERCISE

Goals

    I. To enhance work relationships in intact groups.

    II. To stimulate group discussion about work-related topics.

    III. To clarify assumptions that team members make about each other.

Group Size

Two to twelve. (If the work group is more than twelve, subgroups may be used.)

Time Required

Approximately one hour and a half.

Materials Utilized

Team Development Exercise Question Forms.

Physical Setting

Circle of chairs.

Process

    I. The facilitator introduces the exercise by outlining the goals of the experience. He explains the necessity for openness in work relationships and the need for feedback on one's work style.

    II. The ground rules for the structured experience are explained, one by one. The facilitator checks to see that each member understands the procedure.

    III. Team Development Exercise Question Forms are distributed.

    IV. The facilitator asks members to volunteer to initiate questions. (It may require some prodding by the facilitator for team members to confront specific members. For example, members may be asked to read the list of questions silently and to let one item "float" to the top of their list. When they have centered on one question, they then look around the circle to choose one person to become the focus of the question. Then they volunteer. Some direction from the facilitator may be required for questioners to answer their own queries.)

V. The facilitator interrupts the process after about thirty minutes to assist members in discussing how the exercise is progressing. They may be alerted to the following considerations:

Who questions whom?
How open are we being?
What risks are present in this exercise?
To what degree is trust being generated?
What are we learning about ourselves?
What are we learning about each other?
Whom might you want to do this with privately?
How might we improve the exercise in the next round?

VI. The exercise is resumed, and members are urged to note any change in the process that can be attributed to the processing intervention.

VII. After about twenty minutes the exercise is stopped. The facilitator asks, "If we were to quit right now and never do this again, what question would you regret not having asked someone?" He then invites these questions to be brought out.

VIII. The entire process is critiqued by the team members, and the implications of the exercise for the continued development of the group are discussed. Members may want to plan to use the same questions in a follow-up session some months later.

Variations

I. Team members may be paired in the initial phase to work through as many questions as they can during the time allotted. Then in the second round the risk-taking should be higher. Pairs can be formed on a variety of criteria: boss-subordinate, people who know each other least well, persons who think that they are different from each other.

II. The question form can be supplemented by items suggested by team members.

III. The question form can be generated "from scratch" from items suggested by members of the group. Just before lunch, for example, the team can have a discussion of what they would need to talk about in order to increase openness and trust in their interpersonal relations at work. These items can be duplicated during the meal break for use in the next session.

IV. Members can be asked to write a name or names at the end of each of the

Structured Experience 118

twenty-five questions when they read the list for the first time. This should heighten the volunteering.

V. The process can be interrupted several times in an extended session (2½-3 hours) for members to rate themselves and the team on honesty and risk-taking. The two scales can be displayed on newsprint, and members can record their ratings independently on blank paper.

Dishonest, evasive			ME		Completely honest, open
0	1	2	3	4	5

THE TEAM

Playing it safe			ME		Taking many risks
0	1	2	3	4	5

THE TEAM

Similar Structured Experiences: *Vol. I:* **21;** *Vol. III:* **70;** *Vol. IV:* **116.**
Lecturette Sources: *72 Annual:* "Openness, Collusion, and Feedback"; *73 Annual:* "Johari Window," "Confrontation: Types, Conditions, and Outcomes."

Notes on the use of "Twenty-Five Questions":

Submitted by John E. Jones, University Associates, Iowa City.

TEAM DEVELOPMENT EXERCISE QUESTION FORM

Directions: The list of questions below is designed to stimulate group discussion around work-related topics The following ground rules should govern this discussion:

1. *Take turns asking questions, either to specific individuals or to the group as a whole.*
2. *You must be willing to answer any question which you ask.*
3. *Any member may decline to answer any question which someone else asks.*
4. *Work with the person who is answering to make certain that effective two-way understanding takes place.*
5. *All answers remain confidential within the group.*

QUESTIONS MAY BE ASKED IN ANY ORDER.

1. How do you feel about yourself in your present job?
2. What do you see as the next step in your career development?
3. What personal characteristics do you have that get in the way of your work?
4. What are you doing best right now?
5. What are you trying to get accomplished in your work?
6. Where do you see yourself ten years from now?
7. How are you perceiving me?
8. What would you predict to be my assessment of you?
9. What was your first impression of me?
10. How many different hats do you wear?
11. How do you typically behave when a deadline is approaching?
12. What kind of relationship do you want with me?
13. What things do you do best?
14. What factors in your job situation impede your goal-accomplishment?
15. Whom are you having the most difficulty with right now? (What is that person doing? What is your reaction?)
16. To whom are you closest in your work situation?
17. Where would you locate yourself on a ten-point scale of commitment to the goals of this group (1 is low, 10 is high)?
18. What part are you playing in this group?
19. How do you want to receive feedback?
20. What do you think I'm up to?
21. What puzzles you about me?
22. How are you feeling right now?
23. What issue do you think we must face together?
24. What do you see going on in the group right now?
25. What personal growth efforts are you making?

119. GROUP EXPLORATION: A GUIDED FANTASY

Goals

To allow individuals to share their means of coping with fear and stress as well as their personal responses to pleasure.

Group Size

Six to twelve participants.

Time Required

Approximately one hour.

Materials Utilized

Construction paper, crayons, felt-tipped markers, or other art materials.

Physical Setting

Preferred: carpeted room in which participants can lie down and stretch out comfortably without restricting the space of others.

Process

I. The facilitator invites the group to participate in an exploratory trip. He asks them to make themselves as comfortable as possible and to close their eyes.

II. He explains that he will tell them what is happening on the trip and that they are to listen and fantasize their surroundings and experiences. He tells them that from time to time he will ask them questions. They are to answer these in their own minds, and they will be asked to answer them openly in the group when the experience is over.

III. The following script should be read slowly in a nonabrasive tone of voice:

"We have all gathered together to go down the Colorado River on a raft. We will be led by competent guides, but it will be rough. You must be prepared for a number of critical situations. It will be exciting and pleasurable, but at times it might be painful and dangerous. Contemplate this, consider it, and decide whether you want to go along. If you have some resistance, is there anyone in the group that convinces you to go? How does he or she do it? Do you convince someone else who is reluctant? How do you do it? Whom do you particularly want to go with you on this trip?

"We gather in the boat, our guide at the helm. It is a beautiful day as we start down the river; it is calm and peaceful. In the warm sun, the boat smoothly moving through the waters, you find your mind wandering off. Catch the thought. What are you thinking about? What are you feeling? What reveries do you engage in?

"The boat moves faster, and you see white waters ahead. You are a bit apprehensive, but soon you are in amidst the current. The raft is gently tossed about, but you come through smoothly and easily. This is your first taste of shooting the rapids. As you move down the river, with the cliffs becoming taller and taller on either side of the bank, you find the river moving faster and faster—the white waters becoming more turbulent. You learn that the rapids are rated on a scale from one to ten, and those that you have just gone through are rated two to three. They increase in force, and you are going through rapids rated six and seven. The raft is tossed about, but you cling, getting the excitement and the full taste of the thrill of the waters splashing around you—turning and twisting the raft. You come to a bend in the river, and your guide tells you that the next rapid is scaled ten, but because of the bend in the river it is possible for you to land before reaching the rapids and walk across a spot of land and regain the raft on the other side. You thus have a chance to get off. Do you do so, or do you go on? Do you have a moment of fear? Does anybody convince you to stay on? How? Do you convince anybody else to stay on? How?

"You do go on. The raft is tossed, sometimes tilting at a forty-five degree angle. It turns so that you are going down backwards, then hits a rock and spins around again. Catch the feeling of the turmoil and note your feelings. The twisting and turning diminish. You are out of it and now are moving smoothly and quietly down the waters. What are you feeling?

"Your guide tells you it is time now to rest and seek new adventures, and he lands the raft at the mouth of a blind canyon. He tells you that you will be there for a few hours and that you can explore the canyon. You move into it and find the tall cliffs on either side getting narrower and narrower above you until you are in the middle of a tunnel. It becomes darker and darker. What do you feel? You push on into the blackness, seeing no light behind you or ahead. Do you have any fears? What do you fear?

"Suddenly light shines ahead, and you find yourself at the mouth of a large cave, which is well lighted. The cave is guarded by a gatekeeper, who informs you that there is a treasure within. Each of you has to supply a ticket of ad-

Structured Experience 119

mission—something of yourself which you will give in order to enter the cave. Stop now, open your eyes, and with the material supplied make a ticket, giving something of yourself so that you can proceed."

IV. The facilitator distributes the art materials and allows the participants to draw, write, or in some way construct their "ticket."

V. He continues the fantasy:

"You offer your ticket to the gatekeeper and enter the treasure room. What is your treasure?

"You enjoy your treasure, and then the gatekeeper tells you that you must go on, leaving the treasure behind. What do you feel? You pass out of the cave through a short tunnel and find yourself back on the beach, where your raft has been anchored. With surprise you look behind you and cannot see the crevice out of which you came. The cave is lost. How do you feel?

"Night has now fallen. You see the sky above you up through the canyon; the stars are bright, and a warm breeze engulfs you. The river is flowing swiftly and quietly. You sit around a campfire, reflecting on your adventure, and you think back on all that took place during the day. What does it all mean to you?

"We are now back to today. Here we are in this room. Let us review the answers in your mind."

VI. The facilitator asks various members the answers to each of the questions posed during the fantasy. When he reaches the subject of the ticket of admission, he asks participants to show, discuss, and interact with others concerning what they gave of themselves. The facilitator continues until all of the questions have been dealt with and ends by assisting the group in talking through the impact of the experience.

Variation

The facilitator may use any other fantasy which is appropriate to his particular group, perhaps emphasizing different emotional elements.

Similar Structured Experiences: *Vol. I:* **16;** *72 Annual:* **85;** *73 Annual:* **89.**
Lecturette Source: *72 Annual:* "Communication Modes: An Experiential Lecture."

Submitted by Leo Berman, Hall-Brooke Hospital, Westport, Connecticut.

Notes on the use of "Group Exploration":

120. DIMENSIONS OF TRUST: A SYMBOLIC EXPRESSION

Goals

    I. To explore the various dimensions and meanings of trust.

    II. To promote the creative expression of trust.

Group Size

Any number of groups of five or six participants each.

Time Required

Approximately one hour.

Materials Utilized

    I. Multiple sets of Tinker Toys, Lego Blocks, or similar building toys.

    II. Sheets of 8¼" x 11" paper.

    III. Felt-tipped markers.

    IV. Background instrumental music (optional).

Physical Setting

A room large enough to provide each group with an area in which to work without being disturbed by other groups.

Process

    I. The facilitator may begin with a lecturette on the concept of trust. He focuses on the idea that, although individuals acknowledge the need for trust in relationships, it is often difficult to relate the term to the feelings involved in the expression of trust.

    II. The facilitator forms small groups of five or six participants each. This experience is most effective if the participants in the groups have a previous history together, such as intact work groups or growth groups. If this is not the case, the facilitator should attempt to place individuals into groups in which they know at least some of the members.

III. The facilitator then instructs the groups to concentrate on what elements and feelings are involved in trust and to explore these ideas thoroughly with one another. He tells them that they are to use their materials to build a model which symbolically represents these concepts as they have perceived them. He further asks that they prepare some statement about their model, using the felt-tipped marker and a sheet of newsprint. The facilitator encourages the groups to be expressive and creative in their statements so that what they indicate will aid other groups in understanding the dimensions of trust on which they are focusing.

IV. When all the groups have finished, the facilitator asks each group to make a presentation.

V. The facilitator asks the participants to examine the models of other groups and to note their own reactions to the various concepts that are displayed.

VI. When the participants have finished examining the structures, the facilitator asks them to return to their original groups and to select the one group other than their own that they feel best communicated the concept of trust.

VII. The facilitator assists in the processing of the experience by asking groups to explain why they found the efforts of certain groups to be appealing.

Variations

I. Newsprint can be substituted for the blocks, and groups may be instructed to draw a symbolic representation of trust.

II. The exercise can be preceded by nonverbal trust experiences. (*Vol. I:* 22; *Vol. II:* 44; *Vol. III:* 72.)

III. Key words or phrases from each of the groups may be brought together for a poster that summarizes the major trust concepts that emerged.

IV. Groups can be assigned the task of discussing what behaviors each member can attempt in the remainder of the training event that might enhance inter-personal trust.

Similar Structured Experiences: *Vol. I:* **5, 20;** *Vol. III:* **49;** *73 Annual:* **90;** *Vol. IV:* **101.**
Lecturette Sources: *72 Annual:* "TORI Theory and Practice."

Submitted by James Costigan, Fort Hays Kansas State College.

Notes on the use of "Dimensions of Trust":

121. TOOTHPICKS: AN ANALYSIS OF HELPING BEHAVIORS

Goals

    I. To identify differing approaches to assisting others in a task.

    II. To explore the effects of the various helping approaches on task accomplishment and interpersonal relations.

Group Size

    Ten to twenty participants.

Time Required

    Approximately one hour.

Materials Utilized

    I. Twenty-four toothpicks.

    II. Second puzzle to be held in reserve.

    III. Six instruction cards.

    IV. Pencils for all observers.

    V. Stopwatch or watch with a sweep second hand

Physical Setting

    Room large enough for all observers to see the problem-solvers at work. One table in the center of the room.

Process

    I. The facilitator prepares two puzzles in advance, holding one in reserve in case the first is solved before six trials have been made. Illustrated below is the toothpick puzzle. (Any puzzle which appears difficult enough to last through six trials will be satisfactory.)

Problem: Take away eight toothpicks so that there are only two squares left.

Solution:

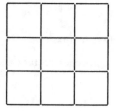

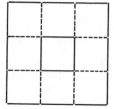

Problem: Connect all nine dots with four straight lines.

Solution·

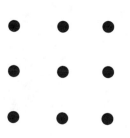

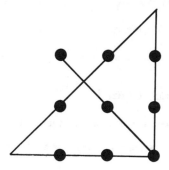

II. The facilitator divides the group into three units for purposes of this experience, according to the number of participants involved. The problem-solvers

should include from one to three participants. The helpers must be exactly six, and the remaining individuals become observers.

III. The problem-solvers are seated at the table, and the helpers leave the room. He then asks the observers to station themselves around the room in such a fashion that they will be able to observe all the action at the table.

IV. The facilitator explains that a puzzle is to be solved and that the observers will be noticing and recording the behaviors of the helpers and the problem-solvers as they work on the puzzle together. He states that the helpers will be allowed into the room one at a time and that each of the six will have one and one-half minutes to assist the problem-solvers.

V. The facilitator then joins the six helpers outside of the room. He briefs the helpers by explaining that they will each have one and one-half minutes to help solve a puzzle which the problem-solvers will be working on at the table. He assigns each a number from one to six, which will be the order in which they will enter the room. He explains that, after each is finished, he will join the observers. He then gives each a card which describes the assisting style which must be used when they are helping with the puzzle. He asks them to keep the information on the card confidential as they wait for their turn to come (**The** facilitator may wish to assign specific styles to particular helpers)

VI. The facilitator returns to the room, places the puzzle on the table, and asks the problem-solvers to wait to begin until the first helper joins them.

VII. The facilitator ushers in the helpers one at a time and allows each exactly one and one-half minutes to assist the problem-solvers.

VIII. After the sixth trial, the facilitator asks the group to process the experience. The problem-solvers report the effects of the various assisting styles on task accomplishment. The observers report how they saw the effects of the various assisting styles on task accomplishment and give descriptions of what they perceived the various styles to be illustrating. The problem-solvers add their perceptions of the differences in the styles.

IX. The facilitator presents a lecturette on the issues of power and influence, calling upon the theoretical material based on the work of French and Raven found in Cartwright and Zander, *Introduction to Group Dynamics,* 2nd ed., Chapter 20. (Evanston, Ill.: Row Peterson, 1962.) The bases of power illustrated by the styles of assistance include: referent, expert, reward, coercive, legitimate, and charismatic. The facilitator asks the group to relate these theories to the experience they have just had and generalize the information to these "bases of power" as they affect relations on the job, in family life, and other situations as the group perceives them. They may also relate these learnings to their experiences within the group.

The following instructions should be written or typed on 3" x 5" cards or slips of paper.

REFERENT

> As you try to help solve the puzzle, show empathy, warmth, familiarity, and liking for the other(s).

EXPERT

> As you try to help solve the puzzle, act like an expert.

REWARD

> As you try to help solve the puzzle, offer encouragement and some reward for successful solution. Promise something good.

COERCIVE

> As you try to help solve the puzzle, urge work at the problem through threats if it is not completed in time.

LEGITIMATE

> As you try to help solve the puzzle, make it clear that you are responsible to your supervisor for the other(s)'s effective work. If this is not immediately clear, keep reminding them.

CHARISMATIC

> As you try to help solve the puzzle, become "personality plus," and hope your enthusiasm and confidence can catch hold.

Variations

I. The six assisting rounds may be videotaped for replay during the processing phase. The tape can be replayed with and without sound, to focus on the interplay between verbal and nonverbal communication.

II. Participants may be asked to "vote" on who played what roles: referent, expert, etc.

Similar Structured Experiences: *Vol. II:* **43**; *Vol. III:* **59, 60.**
Lecturette Source: *72 Annual:* "Defense Mechanisms in Groups"; *73 Annual:* "Helping Relationship Inventory."

Based on materials submitted by Ruth R. Middleman, Temple University, Philadelphia.

Notes on the use of "Toothpicks":

122. EXPRESSING ANGER: A SELF-DISCLOSURE EXERCISE

Goals

I. To study styles of expressing anger in a group setting.

II. To study effects of anger in a group setting.

III. To legitimize the presence and expression of anger within groups.

IV. To identify behaviors which elicit anger in others.

V. To explore ways of coping with anger.

Group Size

From six to twelve participants. Several groups may be directed simultaneously in the same room.

Time Required

Approximately forty-five minutes.

Materials Utilized

I. Felt-tipped markers.

II. Four 3" x 8" strips of paper for each participant.

III. Masking tape.

Physical Setting

Room large enough for participants to move around freely.

Process

I. The facilitator distributes four strips of paper, a felt-tipped marker, and a strip of masking tape to each participant.

II. The facilitator tells the participants that they will be given four sentences to complete, one at a time, and that they are to write down the first response that occurs to them without censoring or modifying the response. He cautions them to print their responses clearly on the newsprint so that others will be able to read them.

III. The facilitator reads the following four sentences, one at a time, allowing for each participant to complete his response. After each sentence is read and the responses have been made, he asks that each participant tape his strip of paper to his chest.

    1. I feel angry when others . . .

    2. I feel that my anger is . . .

    3. When others express anger toward me, I feel . . .

    4. I feel that the anger of others is . . .

IV. The facilitator forms smaller groups of approximately six and asks the participants to process the experience. It is suggested that they focus on the personal impact of sharing their feelings about anger with the group. They are encouraged to give others feedback on the extent to which each individual's responses to anger seem consistent.

V. Generalizations are shared with the entire group. The facilitator may wish to talk about approaches to responding to anger in interpersonal situations.

Variations

I. Participants can be instructed to tape their strips to a wall behind them. Another way is to tape the strips to the back of their chairs.

II. The processing phase may be followed by a practice session on expressing anger. Dyads may be formed to role-play various situations from the history of the group. Members may be urged to explore how they may cope with anger more effectively within the group sessions.

III. The same design can be used with other emotions, such as fright, tenderness, or boredom. Several rounds can be experienced.

IV. Subgroups may be formed of participants who have similar (or highly dissimilar) responses to the four items. Participants can share critical incidents in which they have been involved in which anger was present. Alternative coping behaviors would be discussed.

Similar Structured Experiences: *Vol. I:* **14;** *Vol. III:* **56;** *Vol. IV:* **109, 123;** *'72 Annual:* **75.**
Lecturette Sources: *72 Annual:* "Transcendence Theory," "Notes on Freedom"; *'73 Annual:* "Confrontation: Types, Conditions, and Outcomes."

Submitted by Gary R. Gemmill, School of Management, Syracuse University.

Structured Experience 122

Notes on the use of "Expressing Anger":

123. STRETCHING: IDENTIFYING AND TAKING RISKS

Goals

I. To help participants become aware of interpersonal behavior which is risky for them.

II. To increase participants' awareness of the relationship between risk-taking behavior and the attainment of personal growth goals.

III. To encourage risk-taking behavior as a way of expanding participants' behavioral repertoire.

Group Size

Six to twelve participants, usually the members of an on-going growth group. Several groups may be directed simultaneously in one room.

Time Required

Approximately two hours.

Materials

I. Risk-Taking Behavior in Groups Questionnaire.

II. Pencils.

Physical Setting

Room large enough so that participants can work in dyads and small groups without being disrupted by other groups. An alternative physical setting would be a room large enough to hold all the participants comfortably during the first phases of the experience and several smaller rooms, where individual groups could work undisturbed during the later phases.

Process

I. The facilitator ensures that the participants understand what is meant by risk-taking and the connection between risk-taking and the attainment of personal goals.

II. He then distributes the questionnaire and allows participants time to complete the items.

III. The facilitator asks the participants to form dyads to discuss the questionnaire.

IV. The facilitator may wish to instruct the participants to score their questionnaires and compare overall risk-taking perceptions. He asks that each participant share with his partner the one or two behavioral items from the questionnaire which he considers most risky. Participants are then instructed to share with their partners some of the reasons why they consider these behaviors risky and what they think the consequences of engaging in these behaviors might be. For example, a participant might risk rejection if he expressed sexual attraction toward another member of the group.

V. The facilitator asks the participants to consider how engaging in risk behavior might contribute to their own personal growth goals. The dyad partner should assist in this process.

VI. The participants are then asked to arrive at a decision about whether or not they will engage in a risk behavior in a small group. If they decide they will engage in the behavior, they make a contract with their partner, describing when and under what circumstances they will engage in the behavior.

VII. The facilitator forms small groups of six to twelve participants, leaving dyads intact. He instructs the groups to meet for approximately forty-five minutes. He asks participants to share their risks with each other in this group and to engage in some risky behavior if it is appropriate.

VIII. The facilitator brings the entire group back into a community session to process, integrate, and generalize what has been learned about risk-taking.

Variations

I. After participants have selected the one or two behaviors that would be risky for them, they may be directed in fantasizing those behaviors. The facilitator may ask them to imagine what would be the worst thing that might happen and then what might be the best thing.

II. Each individual may post his score on a piece of newsprint and solicit feedback from the others on how he is perceived in terms of risk-taking behaviors.

III. The group may discuss each item of the questionnaire, attempting consensus on who does and does not display each behavior in the meetings of the group.

IV. Risky situations can be role-played. Persons may volunteer to demonstrate how they might handle various situations.

Similar Structured Experiences: *73 Annual: 99; Vol. IV: 109, 123.*
Lecturette Sources: *72 Annual:* "Risk-Taking and Error Protection Styles"; *73 Annual:* "Risk-Taking."

Notes on the use of "Stretching":

Submitted by Robert Kurtz, University of Iowa, Iowa City

RISK-TAKING BEHAVIOR IN GROUPS QUESTIONNAIRE

Risk-taking behavior in groups is one way of "stretching" yourself to attain personal growth goals. Risk-taking is behavior that ordinarily one would not engage in, that a person would see as posing a possible threat to himself. What constitutes a risk for a person depends on whether it is new behavior for him and whether he has a subjective sense of danger involved in the behavior.

Creative risk-taking in groups can be an effective way to increase the variety of responses you have to different interpersonal situations. With a greater variety of responses available to you, you gain a greater freedom of choice, unrestricted by inhibitions. You have a greater spontaneity of action and more flexibility in your interpersonal relationships.

The purpose of this questionnaire is to ascertain what you would consider risky behavior for yourself in a group situation. Another purpose is to stimulate your thinking with regard to taking risks.

Read the following statements and rate them with regard to how much subjective risk you feel would be involved in this behavior. Use the group you are now in as a reference. Write the appropriate number from the scale below in front of each item.

Would be no risk for me	Would be a small risk for me	I have no feelings one way or the other, or I don't know	Would be some risk for me	Would be a high risk for me
-2	-1	0	+1	+2

_____ 1. Disclosing certain negative feelings about myself to others.

_____ 2. Revealing certain things about my past to others.

_____ 3. Asking for help with my problems from others.

_____ 4. Expressing anger toward someone in the group.

_____ 5. Expressing affection toward someone in the group.

_____ 6. Receiving affection from someone in the group.

_____ 7. Asking for feedback from significant members in the group.

_____ 8. Touching someone else in the group.

_____ 9. Having someone else touch me in the group.

_____ 10. Becoming close and personal with another in front of the group.

_____ 11. Making a statement which might anger someone else in the group.

_____ 12. Expressing and dealing with a conflict I have with another member in the group.

_____ 13. Giving another member negative feedback.

_____ 14. Being the center of attention in the group.

_____ 15. Expressing my confusion and uncertainty in front of the other group members.

_____ 16. Expressing anger or dissatisfaction with the group leader.

_____ 17. Admitting that I was wrong about some other person in the group.

_____ 18. Admitting to the group that I was wrong about an idea that I had.

_____ 19. Talking about sexual feelings in the group.

_____ 20. Sharing a fantasy I have about some member or the total group.

_____ 21. Telling someone in the group that he or she has become very important to me.

_____ 22. Expressing indifference toward other members.

_____ 23. Expressing feelings about another member's physical characteristics.

_____ 24. Talking about my feelings with regard to my physical characteristics in the group.

_____ 25. Admitting that someone had hurt my feelings in the group.

_____ 26. Telling the group members to leave me alone, to "get off my back."

_____ 27. Walking out of the group while under stress.

_____ 28. Expressing sexual attraction toward another member in the group.

124. THE IN-GROUP: DYNAMICS OF EXCLUSION

Goals

  I. To allow participants to experience consciously excluding and being excluded.

 II. To confront feelings which exclusion generates.

III. To examine processes by which social identity is conferred by the excluding group and accepted by the excluded member.

Group Size

Unlimited number of small groups of five or six participants each.

Time Required

Approximately one-and-a-half hours.

Materials Utilized

Refreshments, such as cold drinks and snacks.

Physical Setting

Room large enough so that groups can work without disturbing each other.

Process

  I. The facilitator forms small groups of five or six participants each and asks the groups to be seated on the floor, leaving some distance between groups.

 II. The facilitator directs each group to exclude some member based upon criteria consensually devised by the group. He tells the groups that they have twenty minutes to perform this task. When each excluded member has been selected, he is sent to a predetermined place in the room.

III. After each group has excluded a member and the excluded participants are seated in the special place provided for them, the facilitator tells everyone except those who were excluded to take a fifteen-minute refreshment break. He instructs those taking a break not to communicate with or include, in any way, the members of the excluded group during this time.

IV. Following the refreshment break, the facilitator asks the groups to reassemble and quickly choose a spokesman. Excluded members may not rejoin their groups at this time. He then asks the excluded group to locate in the center of the room and the nonexcluded groups to form around this group in clusters so that each group remains intact.

V. The facilitator asks each member of the excluded group to tell why he was excluded from the group, whether he feels that the exclusion was justified, how he feels about the group that excluded him, and how he feels about the other excluded members.

VI. After each excluded participant has spoken, the facilitator asks the spokesman from each excluding group to tell what their criteria were for excluding and why they felt that the excluded member met the criteria.

VII. When each spokesman has finished, the original groups are reassembled, including excluded members. Their task is to react to the content of the previous phases.

VIII. The facilitator then asks the participants to form one large group. He presents a lecturette on the dynamics of exclusion, emphasizing aspects of social identity, characteristics of interactions between "stigmatized" persons and "normals," and characteristics of interactions among "stigmatized" persons. Following the lecturette, the total group is engaged in processing the experience in terms of the theory input.

Variations

I. A process observer may be assigned to the excluded group to make notes on the extent to which they develop cohesion. He might be sensitized to the cliche, "Misery loves company."

II. Excluded members can be designated by some object, such as hats, arm bands, special name tags. They may be asked to retain this designation throughout the continuing process of group life to ascertain if the excluding dynamics persist beyond the original experience.

III. Activities other than a refreshment break can be planned, such as playing energetic games or watching a movie in a different room.

IV. In step IV of the process, the spokesmen may assemble in the center rather than members of the excluded group. The excluded members could be told to wait on the side until the spokesmen complete their discussion.

V. After step I V the small groups may be reassembled, with excluded members outside their circles. The excluded members are to break into these circles to re-include themselves. As soon as each excluded member has penetrated the circle, his group processes the exercise.

Similar Structured Experience: *Vol. I:* **17.**
Lecturette Sources: *73 Annual:* "Dependency and Intimacy," "Confrontation: Types, Conditions, and Outcomes."

Notes on the use of "The In-Group":

Submitted by Gale Goldberg, Temple University, Philadelphia.

CONTRIBUTORS

Chip Bell
Training Director
North Carolina National Bank
P. O. Box 120
Charlotte, North Carolina 28201

Leo H. Berman
Director of Professional Services
Hall-Brooke Hospital
Westport, Connecticut 06880

Meyer M. Cahn
Professor of Higher Education
San Francisco State College
1600 Holloway Avenue
San Francisco, California 94132

Mary Carson
Cedar Rapids Community Schools
Cedar Rapids, Iowa 52404

James Costigan
Chairman, Department of Speech
Fort Hays Kansas State College
Hays, Kansas 67601

Ann Dew
South East Junior High School
2501 Bradford Drive
Iowa City, Iowa 52240

Lawrence Dunn
Director of Program Planning
   and Development
Training and Development
   Systems, Ltd.
25 Huntington Avenue
Boston, Massachusetts 02116

Ord Elliott
University Associates
P. O. Box 615
Iowa City, Iowa 52240

Gary R. Gemmill
Associate Professor of
   Organizational Behavior
Syracuse University School of
   Management
116 College Place
Syracuse, New York 13210

Gale Goldberg
Assistant Professor
School of Social Administration
Temple University
Philadelphia, Pennsylvania 19122

Brant Holmberg
Pacific Lutheran University
Tacoma, Washington 98447

Tom Irwin
Counseling Center
Virginia Polytechnic Institute
Blacksburg, Virginia 24601

Johanna Jones
1405 Sycamore
Iowa City, Iowa 52240

Ronald D. Jorgenson
Pacific Lutheran University
Tacoma, Washington 98447

Beverly Kaye
Leadership Institute for
  Community Development
Suite 600
2021 L. Street, N.W.
Washington, D.C. 40036

Donald Keyworth
Professor of Philosophy
Drake University
Des Moines, Iowa 50311

Robert Kurtz
Counseling Center
Iowa Memorial Union
Iowa City, Iowa 52241

John Linhardt
Leadership Institute for
  Community Development
Suite 600
2021 L. Street, N.W.
Washington, D.C. 40036

L. A. Mike McKeown
Leadership Institute for
  Community Development
Suite 600
2021 L. Street, N.W.
Washington, D.C. 40036

Richard J. McLean
Leadership Institute for
  Community Development
Suite 600
2021 L. Street, N.W.
Washington, D.C. 40036

Ferdinand Maire
Bureau de Psychologie Industrielle
2068 Hauterive
Switzerland

Ruth R. Middleman
School of Social Administration
Temple University
Philadelphia, Pennsylvania 19122

Suzanne Pavletich
South East Junior High School
2501 Bradford Drive
Iowa City, Iowa 52240

Morton S. Perlmutter
Associate Professor
Director, Multimethods-Video
  Laboratory
School of Social Work
425 Henry Mall
Madison, Wisconsin 53706

Bud Rainbow
Cedar Rapids Community Schools
Cedar Rapids, Iowa 52404

Anthony Reilly
Director, Human Resource
  Development and Consultation
University Associates
1712 N. Illinois Street
Indianapolis, Indiana 46202

John J. Sherwood
Krannert Graduate School of
  Industrial Administration
Purdue University
Lafayette, Indiana 47907

Tom White
Cedar Rapids Community Schools
Cedar Rapids, Iowa 52404

Robert T. Williams
Assistant Professor
Department of Education
Colorado State University
Fort Collins, Colorado 80521

David Zellinger
Krannert Graduate School of
    Industrial Administration
Purdue University
Lafayette, Indiana 47907

Amy M. Zelmer
Assistant Professor
Corbett Hall
The University of Alberta
82 Avenue and 112 Street
Edmonton 7, Alberta, Canada

SOURCES OF ADDITIONAL
STRUCTURED EXPERIENCES

Gunther, B. *Sense Relaxation: Below Your Mind*. New York: Collier Books, 1968.

Gunther, B. *What to Do Till the Messiah Comes*. New York: Collier Books, 1971.

Jones, J.E., and J.W. Pfeiffer. *The 1973 Annual Handbook for Group Facilitators*. Iowa City: University Associates, 1973.

Lewis, H., and H. Streitfield. *Growth Games*. New York: Bantam, 1971.

Maier, N.R.F., A.R. Solem, and A.A. Maier. *Supervisory and Executive Development: A Manual for Role Playing*. New York: Wiley, 1967.

Malamud, D.I., and S. Machover. *Toward Self-Understanding: Group Techniques in Self-Confrontation*. Springfield, Ill.: Thomas, 1965.

NTL Institute for Applied Behavioral Science. *Twenty Exercises for Trainers*. Washington, D.C., 1972.

Nylen, D., J.R. Mitchell, and A. Stout (eds.). *Handbook of Staff Development and Human Relations Training: Materials Developed for Use in Africa* (rev. ed.). Washington, D.C.: NTL Institute for Applied Behavioral Science, 1967.

Otto, H.A. *Group Methods to Actualize Human Potential: A Handbook* (2nd ed.). Beverly Hills: Holistic Press, 1970.

Pfeiffer, J.W., and R. Heslin, *Instrumentation in Human Relations Training: A Guide to 75 Instruments with Wide Application to the Behavioral Sciences*. Iowa City: University Associates, 1973.

Pfeiffer, J.W., and J.E. Jones. *A Handbook of Structured Experiences for Human Relations Training. Volumes I, II, III*. Iowa City: University Associates, 1969, 1970, 1971.

Pfeiffer, J.W., and J.E. Jones. *The 1972 Annual Handbook for Group Facilitators*. Iowa City: University Associates, 1972.

Satir, V. *Conjoint Family Therapy: A Guide to Theory and Technique*. Palo Alto, Cal.: Science and Behavior Books, 1967.

Schutz, W.C. *Joy: Expanding Human Awareness*. New York: Grove Press, 1967.